CHEERS FR

It is an honor to share my thoughts on this amazing book. First and foremost, I have always known Coach Roz to be an incredible man of character. He is truly a gifted motivational speaker, and a master at engaging an audience, young and old. I should not have been surprised when I learned he was the author of several books. The construction of this book meshes perfectly with his organization, and lends itself successfully to the many topics surrounding why the Playmakers curriculum and mission statement are crucial for coaches, kids, educators, mothers, and fathers. This book transcends the X's and O's and deals with the real issues concerning youth sports programs and the substandard teaching practices that are not necessarily in the best interests of our youth. This book managed to surpass my high expectations and encompasses the best of Coach Roz.

Jeff Penn, Executive Director
Cops 4 Kids & Communities, Southern California

I am always listening for the voices that take me deeper, help me lift others higher, and keep me focused on what matters right now. "Coach Roz" is one of those voices. He is one of the few men in my life who doesn't have to tell me WHY I should read a certain book, or listen to a particular talk, or meet someone, or go someplace. Coach Roz says - Glenn Tobias does. He's earned that with me.

So when Coach Roz tells you that the camps he and Harrison Phillips will be running will change your mindset, improve your skills, and exponentially multiply your impact, please listen! I assure you, you will be grateful you did.

Read this book, follow the practical advice herein, get to the camps regularly, and then enjoy having an impact in the lives of others like you may never have realized was possible before.

Glenn Tobias, Former Pastor, Co-Director of The Forge Men's Ministry
Reston, Virginia

As an Executive Coach to the top leaders of major organizations around the country, I can spot great leaders with an inspiring and important mission, and that describes Coach Roz and Playmakers. Transformational coaching is what Coach Roz and Playmakers is all about. While effectively teaching sound football skills, character-shaping is the primary focus of Playmakers. In this, his most recent book, with humor, passion, and great storytelling, Coach Roz reveals the true humility, curiosity, and dedication to the betterment of kids that describe both him and his hopes for the coaches he trains. I have known this man for a number of years and he is the real deal. I whole-heartedly endorse Playmakers and the important work it is doing in helping to strengthen our next generation of leaders.

Michael E. Zacharia, Executive Coach
Folsom, California

When I began coaching nine years ago, I had no Head Coaching experience. Fortunately, I met Greg Roeszler, and he changed my life.

Many times, when faced with a difficult situation or decision, I would ask myself what Coach Roz would do, and it has never failed to help me do things the right way. Since then, we have won two Deaf Prep National Championships, won the Section GPA Pennants three times, been featured on television often, and improved immensely in student-athlete character.

His camps are always free. Somehow he always finds a place for our team (who lives two hours away) to stay overnight, and he always provides food for our hungry boys. The best part about his camps is how he speaks to others. He always stresses the importance of brotherhood, caring for others, proper safe football drills, and character. I speak from experience when I say his heart is gold.

Coach Roz is a coach for all coaches, and his Playmakers Camps are some of my student-athletes' favorite memories. I am proud to call him a true friend! Please enjoy this book as much as I have enjoyed working with Roz. It will change your life!

Warren Keller, Athletic Director and Head Football Coach
California School for the Deaf, Fremont, California

Society today is way different than it was when I first started coaching 27 years ago. Kids have challenges and difficulties today that were not even invented 30 years ago. This book will give coaches the edge by showing you how to develop uncommon student-athletes whose focus is on the importance of doing what is right, not what is popular.

If you want uncommon players, you must first become an uncommon coach. This book will give you a game plan on how to re-develop yourself as a husband, father, teacher, and coach, and it will show you and your coaching staff how to practice what you preach.

I was with Coach Roz at the start of Playmakers in Omaha 10 years ago and used his teachings and strategies in my program at Omaha Burke. It has proven to be very successful. We are an inner-city school that focuses on faith, community, and brotherhood. We have all the same problems as any other city school. Our edge is we have coaches who build lifelong relationships with kids because they care deeply about a player's full development, both on and off the playing field. This past season, 11 out of 16 seniors have earned scholarships to play college football next year. This stat has more to do with love, encouragement, and accountability than it does football talent.

I urge all coaches to read this book, but more importantly, to challenge yourself to use these strategies to become better - not only as a coach, but as a man of faith.

Paul Limongi, Head Football Coach,
2018 USA Today Nebraska Football Coach of the Year
Burke High Bulldogs, 2018 Class A State Champions, Omaha, Nebraska

Coach Roz has really "outkicked his coverage" with his latest book. Through this book, Roz is visibly raw, transparent, and sincere with his emotions, ultimately inspiring others to be open, honest, and genuine with themselves and the youth they serve.

Coach Roz has always had a heart for the at-risk youth and the unique issues they are exposed to. Long before the formal creation of the Playmakers Organization, Roz was on the front lines caring deeply for the underprivileged. Now, with the needed visibility and partnerships with other Playmakers and organizations around the US, Playmakers and Coach Roz are poised to make a tremendous positive impact on generations of young men and women.

One cannot ask of another what one is unwilling to do on their own. Roz leads us all by demonstrating the qualities needed to impact our youth and the communities in which we should all be serving.

Grant Moyer, President, Momentum Fitness Solutions
Houston, Texas

When I first started coaching, my goal was to dominate football games with players who were stronger than any of our opponents. Then I heard Coach Roz say, "Someday these guys will be done with football, but for the rest of their lives they will be men, fathers, husbands, employees, and important to our communities. What you can teach them about character is what they will take with them." Character development has been an important part of my practice planning and season goals ever since. Coach Roz has a talent for inspiring and motivating people to remember what is truly most important.

Shannon Sauer, Head Varsity Football Coach
Tracy Buccaneers Football Organization, Tracy, California

As a longtime volunteer coach for young people, I know the importance of utilizing sports as an opportunity to teach young people the importance of academic excellence, character development, and leadership skills. These attributes are critical to the success of our young people, who often are not exposed to positive adult male role models. The success of our "Youth of Promise" is a critical factor in building families and communities for the future. I have watched Playmakers do just that here in Omaha. I'm excited to see what the future holds for this great organization.

John W. Ewing, Jr., Douglas County Treasurer
Omaha, Nebraska

Coach Roz and Harrison Phillips have put together a Playbook for anyone in a leadership capacity that shows how to put faith-based leadership principles into their everyday game plan. The making of an Uncommon Man, as Coach Roz details, gives coaches a path that will help develop the character of young men and women, inspiring them to become faith-based leaders in their lives.

Thanks to men like Coach Roz and Harrison Phillips for all they do for the High Risk and Special Needs children in our communities!

Coach Craig Millius, Screaming Eagles Athletics
Omaha, Nebraska

To Jareome

Do not be afraid, God has his hands all over you.
Your Aunt Billie will be there, and Coach will be there, too.
You know I can't have favorites,
but you know I love you, the most.
You are my Noodlehead.

BEYOND COACHING

Building Character and Leadership

Greg "Coach Roz" Roeszler
Harrison Phillips, Buffalo Bills
with Donna Miesbach

PLAYMAKERS PRESS ™
Folsom, California

© 2020 Greg Roeszler, Harrison Phillips, and Donna Miesbach. All rights reserved. No part of this book may be used or reproduced in any manner whatsoever without written permission except in the case of brief quotations embodied in critical articles or reviews. Any similarities to other intellectual works are either coincidental or have been properly cited when the source is known. Trademarks of products, services, and organizations mentioned herein belong to their respective owners and are not affiliated with Playmakers Press.

The names of some of the students mentioned in this book may have been changed. Their stories have not.

Paperback: 978-0-9822514-7-8
Kindle: 978-0-9822514-8-5
EPUB: 978-0-9822514-9-2
Library of Congress Cataloging Number 2020914059
Cataloging in Publication Data on file with publisher.

Playmakers Press
A Division of Playmakers Mentoring Foundation
2795 E. Bidwell St, Suite 100
Folsom, CA 95630
(916) 220-1284
E-mail: CoachRoz@ThePlaymakers.org

Editorial Services: Donna Miesbach
Marketing & Publicity: Concierge Marketing, Inc.

Printed in the United States of America
10 9 8 7 6 5 4 3 2 1

CONTENTS

Foreword — xi
Introduction — 1

PART ONE - UNCOMMON COACHING

Faith and Football — 9
Meeting "Bigfoot" — 17
"It's Different" — 27
The Future — 41
Something Larger Than Myself — 59

PHOTO ALBUM — 73

PART TWO - TACKLING LIFE

Introduction — 91
Relationship with Roz and Jordan — 93
Why Playmakers—A Nonprofit with God at the Center — 99
Shortcomings — 101
Why I Am Passionate About Paying It Forward — 109
Faith — 113
Kids with Special Needs — 117
Coaching — 125
Conclusion — 133

PART THREE - RESOURCES

Invite Coach Roz to Speak to Your Group! — 137
Coaching for Character Clinics — 139
Free Summer Football Camps — 141
Partnering with Playmakers — 143
About Playmakers Books — 145
Order More Books — 147
Acknowledgments — 149
About the Authors — 151

FOREWORD

The world seems determined to keep running off the rails. In virtually every arena of life, we are regularly reminded of the chaos that has become the norm. Sports is no exception. One day it is another disturbing story of a professional athlete whose fame and fortune corrupted their character and produced devastating results. The next day it is the parent of a little leaguer punching a volunteer umpire because ball four was called instead of strike three. The following day a frustrated old coach is fired for mistreating his players. The stories are increasingly common and point to core problems in our culture, our values, and in the overall state of the human soul.

I have known Greg Roeszler for a long time. Coach "Roz" is a friend and fellow coach who continues to examine his inner world in the hope of unearthing the issues that God wants to transform and heal. In addition, Coach Roz is a man and a coach who has invested his time, energy, and skill into using the arena of sports to cultivate men and women of character who will positively influence the world long after their playing days are over.

Winning in terms of the scoreboard has always been too small of a goal for Greg. For as long as I have known him, he has been passionate about developing coaches and players who have world-class character. Long before it was fashionable to care about such things, Greg was working to inspire coaches to care more about building great people than great players.

In light of where our world is, and where it continues to be heading, coaches need a book like this one to remind them of what ultimately matters and what doesn't. A book like this provides a foundation for coaches to reconsider their role as shapers and influencers of those whose athletic career will soon end, but whose character will continue for a lifetime and impact generations.

It is a privilege to be entrusted with a group of athletes who look to us to help them succeed in sports, but coaching football - or baseball - or soccer is more of a calling to influence young people to be lifelong pursuers of high character. This is the heartbeat of Coach "Roz" and Playmakers. This is the heart of this book. Read it at your own risk, because it will inspire you to be a better coach — and along the way you might begin to realize the scoreboard that really matters, and the one that doesn't!

Pastor Mike Lueken, Senior Pastor
Oak Hills Church, Folsom, California

INTRODUCTION

MAKING A DIFFERENCE

When you have never known your father, how can you know what a father should act like? When you have never had a family, how can you know what that means? And when you have had to fend for yourself all your young life, who can you look to for a role model? Who is there to teach you what it means to have real character, to be responsible, and yes, to take care of yourself and others, too? How does one learn to be a good citizen, even a leader in the community, when your entire life has been based on survival?

This is the predicament so many of our young people face, but because there are those who care, a way out is being carved in the streets and slums of our inner cities. Because there are those who care, a "family" is being formed where kids can feel safe, where they are not only respected, but loved. In the shelter of these "families," coaches who care stand both as role models and surrogate fathers for these lost children. As they do, they teach the kids what community service means so they can learn to reach beyond themselves.

As the kids learn how to serve, a sense of pride and responsibility, and, yes, leadership begins to grow in their young hearts. Now they can hold their heads up high. Because they know now why there are rules, abiding by those rules becomes a source of pride. Now they know it is by working together that they all can succeed. And when one of them happens to stray, as we all do at some time or other, the lessons of leadership and compassion take on real meaning for those young compatriots who help them find their way back.

Integrity becomes a word with meaning, a word that defines how they are trying to live their lives. Integrity becomes the gold standard for these budding citizens, for they are learning through their own experience that those who live with integrity live well, regardless of the circumstances in which life has placed them.

Because the kids are trying, because they are sincere, dreams begin to form. "Maybe I can go to college someday. If I work hard enough, maybe that will be possible."

"No," the coaches tell them. "Not maybe. You will. If you can dream it, you can do it," and so the dream grows. Horizons broaden. Their world and their vision are no longer confined by the streets of the inner city, no longer threatened by gang rule. They have found a way out because someone cared.

Unfortunately, too many of our youth are caught in this maze, but the good news is that people who care are doing something about it all over the nation. Mentoring groups are springing up wherever you turn. Coaches are dedicating their lives to providing shelter and guidance for those who need it. The wheel is turning slowly, but it is turning. Lives are being changed. Dreams are being realized. More and more we all are learning that life is about helping each other.

So why were we surprised when kids with special needs appeared on our horizon? What a joy it is to have them under our umbrella now, too! They are taking our work to another level and adding a richness to our program that we hadn't anticipated. Our hearts are growing, right along with our outreach.

Serving kids is what Playmakers is all about. We invite you to join us.

Donna Miesbach,
Retired Omaha Coordinator & Assistant to Coach Roz
Co-author of Playmakers Books, Omaha, Nebraska

A WORD FROM THE SIDE LINES

Being Harrison's parents, we were involved with Playmakers since 2015 when Harrison was at Stanford, so we fully understand what Playmakers is about—their mission statement, their core values, and the struggles they experience getting programs started and running. We especially recognize and admire the extremely positive impact they have not just on the kids, but on the community as well. And we love Greg and Linda! They took our son, as if their own, and provided fellowship and some good hot meals when he needed them.

When Coach Roz provided us with the opportunity to read this manuscript prior to printing, we tried to read this through the eyes of someone like you who, perhaps, doesn't know Coach Roz, or who has never heard of this organization. We believe Greg has done a great job outlining the Playmakers concept and making his point.

The one recurring thought we had while reading this was how different this coaching strategy is—it almost makes one a little uncomfortable. Having raised Harrison and his sister, Delanie (an athlete in her own right in four different sports through the college level), we have been exposed to so many coaching styles—from "dad" coaches, to high school, to college, and now to professional. All of these varied a little, based on the coach's personality or the team's mission, but they all had one main goal: to build a better team and WIN.

And now here is Playmakers with a faith-based style whose goal is not to win, but to mentor kids so they gain a sense of self-worth, giving them reasons to take pride in themselves, to learn respect—above all - for others, and to feel a sense of inclusion when they may have been passed by or not even given a chance to participate or belong!

We have witnessed the Playmakers in action, tearing up as we watched 150 developmentally different kids get to "play ball," most for the first time, when Harrison and the Playmakers offered their free camp in Omaha in 2019. And it wasn't just football! The local police brought their horse patrol and their canines to do a presentation. The Fire Department brought a fire truck for the kids to tour—and were they ever impressed with the height that ladder extended to! A DJ played music throughout the camp, so we all got to dance a lot, too. Awards were given out in several categories, which made the winners sooooo proud!

We can't express the unbridled joy we saw that day—a little girl with cerebral palsy scoring a touchdown—three young boys with Down syndrome climbing on Harrison like a jungle gym and then bombing him with water balloons! The day warmed our hearts and changed us.

The camps would not have been possible without the support of local sponsors. Yes, it took a little effort to get Omaha's camp up and running, but every 2019 sponsor doubled their support for 2020, and other potential sponsors are reaching out to us. They all saw something special, and want to be part of it. Their participation is just a testament to what Playmakers does.

To make it even better, the same things are happening in Sacramento and Buffalo! Harrison's Playmakers in Buffalo have the advantage of Harrison living there. He does not want his connection with them to be a "one and done" thing. He believes providing a consistent, repetitive, and positive relationship with them will have a much deeper, more meaningful impact. This means they have had pizza parties, bowling nights, basketball tournaments, a night at Dave and Busters, and Harrison even got THEM to learn to pay it forward when they themselves donated toys and delivered them to the Children's Hospital.

Whether or not you decide to reach out to Coach Roz for a coach's clinic, we hope you will consider utilizing the philosophies and techniques he presents in this book. Not only can you make the world a better place, but you may be surprised at how good you feel watching it all happen.

As you read Greg's book, you will get an opinion of him, so let me tell you up front—he is a dreamer who operates at 30,000 feet. Anything is possible, and nothing will stop him. When he does descend to the weeds and muddy details where we all live, he helps take on the challenges. His faith sustains his belief in his purpose.

In 2015, Roz didn't know that in five short years, Playmakers would extend from Sacramento 1600 miles East to Omaha, and then another 2500 miles East to Buffalo, New York. Now that they have, he wants to know, "Why not have a Playmakers group in every NFL city?"

Yes, he's at 30,000 feet again—but why not?

Paul and Tammie Rose Phillips
Omaha, Nebraska

PART ONE

UNCOMMON COACHING

BY
COACH GREG ROESZLER

~1~

FAITH AND FOOTBALL

LIFE ON THE ROZ TRAIN

When I began writing this book, I wasn't 100% sure what the result was going to look like. All I knew for sure was that it was Harrison's idea that we write one, and that seemed like a good idea. There were several challenges to this, including the fact that he is 3,000 miles away at the tail end of his second year with the Buffalo Bills, and is rehabbing his knee. We were also looking at doing our Buffalo camp on May 9th, and I have put a ridiculous time frame on this to have the book ready when we do the camp. I do know that I need to trust the process, abandon the outcome, and "come up shootin'…" Welcome to my world.

WHEN THE GAME LEAVES YOU

A couple of years ago, I had the opportunity to speak to a college football team through the invitation of my friend, Ted Popson. Ted is one of the finest men that I know. He played for several years as a tight end in the NFL, ending his career with the 49ers. Over the years, Ted and I have become tremendous friends, and I respect him so much. This was one of those speaking opportunities where I did not know exactly what I was going to say to the team, so I had to trust the process as it unfolded. I found myself standing in front of 75 players and 10 coaches when Ted introduced me. I began by giving them an example of how football was like dating a very, very beautiful woman. I asked them to imagine what it looked like and felt like to have this beautiful woman walking around the campus with them and joining in all the social activities there.

While most of them were able to relate to that immediately, I'm sure they were curious about where this was going, and so was I. Then it struck me that we have all been in relationships that have ended too early. So what I said next was to imagine that the girl who brings you so much joy dumps you before you are ready to be dumped. What does that feel like? Do you feel betrayed or ripped off? That you didn't get what you deserved?

Almost all young people can relate to that. Too often that is how we leave football. It's something we love, something that brings us much joy, yet it leaves us on its terms, not ours.

Over the years, many former football players have talked with me about how the game wronged them and how they felt cheated. Their playing time was shortened because of "political reasons," or "the coach didn't like them." There was one reason after another that left a bad taste in that player's mouth.

How unfortunate that the game we love just ended too soon for us. We feel the game abandoned us. As I was telling this story, each coach was nodding his head over how the game had left him too soon. The point I tried to get across to these young men was to live in integrity and take full advantage of the game and that relationship. Develop quality relationships now, mentor and help others, and be the best man that you possibly can while the game is current and has not left you.

I believe that message helped some of the kids who were in the room that day. It certainly affected the coaches who were listening. Maybe it even got them thinking about how they coach their kids. It certainly was beneficial for me, as it helped me exorcise some of the demons that I have about the game and how it left me. It was funny how my speaking to a group would help me work out my own frustrations.

A CONFESSION

The beautiful and ugly part of this game is what it exposes about our soul. If we're willing to dig down beneath the surface, one of the things the game exposes for many of us is pride. In my case, underneath the category of pride comes performance and approval. Here's an example of how pride played itself out when I was a young man. When I was at a community college before I attended San Diego State, I was the starting quarterback, I kicked field goals, and I punted. That is three positions that I played in community college. For some, that would be good enough, but not for me and my pride. Then, when I was at San Diego State, I had the good fortune to qualify for two positions - one was quarterback, and the other was punter. However, I never had the opportunity to start as a quarterback because of three arm surgeries, so I was the starting punter for both my junior and senior year at San Diego State.

For many people, the accomplishment of being a Division 1 college punter should have been more than enough. Not so with me. When people would ask me what position I played, first I would say, "quarterback," second was "a punter." Big deal, you might think? Looking back now, I would have to say not so much, but I didn't feel that way then. Over the years, I have found that many people have felt that way, too.

For years, my soul was restless because I never accomplished being a starting Division One quarterback. That frustration manifested itself in many ways later in life. To this day, I have recurring dreams about football. Most of them, not pleasant. Rarely did I enjoy or celebrate the fact that I was one of the better Division One punters in college football. In my mind, being a punter was not center stage. It did not bring my ego enough gratification. Pride in my performance and seeking the approval of others has been a theme of mine, not just in my business career but in my relationships with others, too. It was only after I began my journey of faith that I would let those doors be opened so I could safely poke around inside and allow healing to occur. I believe that through those exercises I have become a better man, a better husband, and a better coach.

As you take this example and move it into coaching today, I have begun to identify some themes that can help us be better coaches. How did those themes make me a better coach? They helped me understand how kids think today, and what might be going on in their souls. For example, an oversized roly-poly kid who immediately gets put on the line because of his weight. A father who played running back and therefore believes his son needs to play running back, too.

I often have to ask myself if my pride is getting in the way when I'm interacting with an athletic director or other authority figures that I must submit to. "Submit" is an interesting word. It tastes like vinegar in most of our mouths, particularly to us testosterone-filled coaches. To tell the truth, the theme of pride-performance-approval runs through all of my relationships, not just coaching. I believe that if I stay diligent in the pursuit of eliminating pride and performance approval from my life, not only will I be a better man, husband, and father, but I will be a better coach as well.

HOW THE BOOK IDEA CAME ABOUT

The last time I saw Harrison was in Buffalo when a youth foundation invited us to speak to a group of over 100 youth and high school coaches, so I was looking forward to this trip. Most of the time, I am quite comfortable in front of a group. This was a little different since the group included Hall of Fame running back Thurman Thomas, David Egner (CEO of the Bills Foundation), as well as a local kids foundation that both Harrison and I wanted to partner with in Buffalo.

The setting was pretty cool. It was in a suite in the Buffalo Bills' New Era Stadium that catered to and seated about 200, including people from the Bills' front office, the Bills' Charitable Foundation people, one of the most influential youth mentoring organizations in Buffalo, some corporate people, and many athletes whom I have watched for years. I was there because of the relationship that a volunteer coach (me) had with a young man who was in the prime of his football career and with his life yet to live. So there I was, getting ready to speak alongside Harrison to a group of coaches, just like me. Who would have thought that such possibilities exist? I am 3,000 miles from home, in an NFL venue, and someone thinks I have something to say.

Having spoken to large groups usually excites me. I know surveys have been done by some pretty smart people which show that, for some folks, public speaking is a fear greater than death. That may or may not be an exaggeration, but I think the point is made. It scares some people. It just is not my biggest fear.

There are two ways that I prepare to speak in public settings. One is to script every sentence and leave nothing to error. That tends to keep my emotions more in check. I am a very emotional person and can cry at the drop of a hat, or at least about things I am passionate about. That always includes mentoring and relationships. The other way I prepare is the opposite of that, which is to "just wing it." I could really "church that up" and say that I'm being led by the Holy Spirit. I am not sure if that is what it really is, or me just liking the high wire of winging it. In any case, this event was far more on the "wing it" side, as I did not know how the flow was going to go when there were variables beyond what I can usually control.

Here I am, a 63-year-old, marginally educated San Diego State Aztec. That is important, because Harrison and Stanford played the Aztecs his last year in college, and the Aztecs whupped Stanford. I told him that was going to happen. This has little to do with our book or our clinics, but it is fun reminding him that we kicked his tail. So there I am in Buffalo, my expenses paid, including a 5-star hotel, and meeting some tremendous people, all because I am a volunteer coach who works with tough, at-risk kids and kids with special needs through football.

DARKER TRUTHS

Events like this usually create some faith conflicts with me. In the 22 years that I have been a Christ follower, I have learned much about my two addictions, performance and approval, which are rooted in pride. Speaking at an event such as this feeds both of those addictions. The ugly truth is, I want to speak in such a manner that everyone will think I am a tremendous speaker and loves what I have to say. Let me go a step further—deep down I want them to tell me that as well. I also want to impress Harrison. I am embarrassed to admit this to you, but it is the truth. Welcome to the darker side of "Coach Roz."

The challenge that I have is my two addictions cannot be satisfied. For me, there can never be too much performance and approval, and for much of my life, that has been what has kept me from living the life that was designed for me. I love living on the high wire.

If we are willing to investigate the motives for why we coach, some of the darker truths come to the surface. So often I hear coaches say they coach to mentor kids. They say they want to teach kids to be men, or the really dangerous one: "I want my son to have 'good coaching.'" On the surface, these can be good motives. This game does teach life lessons. It can nurture true masculinity and create amazing life friendships. The problem is that you can shadow some coaches on the field or during a game and find little to no evidence of those noble motives. If they are not being taught on the practice field or in game situations, where are they being taught?

This book, and the clinics that my friend and mentor, Harrison Phillips, and I are writing and conducting, hit these tough coaching/mentoring topics head on. Yes, I say "mentor" when I describe Harrison. This young man that God has put in my path is teaching this now 63-year-old coach much about life. Harrison holds me to a higher standard by bringing me closer to Christ and making me look at the areas of my character that need shaping.

So I guess that is what this book/clinic will be about. It is a book that openly speaks of our faith in our awesome God. That is "fairly" safe so far. We will also talk about how we attempt to live the lives Christ has modeled for us. Getting dangerous now. We will look at and discuss our addictions, shortcomings, and where we are challenged to be shaped even more, and still grow as Christ followers. Then we will mix in the subject of our true masculinity and where sports, and particularly our football experiences, have shaped that, for good or bad. (Is anyone still in the room?) Finally, we are going to offer our coaching clinics to men who are willing to come and explore those subjects. If we sell 30 books and get 10 coaches to show up, it will be a miracle. Keep in mind that the Carpenter from Nazareth got quite a bit accomplished with 12 ragtag fishermen, which history reports were an average age of under 30.

Imagine a coaching book and clinic where you were coming to learn and collaborate on how to shape young men. Where you, as a coach, left a better man. Where it was not only discussed, but was taken to the field where it could be repeated. Imagine a practice plan that was organized in such a way that time was spent on character development and life lessons. A practice field where organization was key; where coaches used coaching whistles and were dressed in practice coaching attire, not blue jeans. Well, this is what Harrison and I have aspired to do. We are going to journey together and see who really wants to join us. My big goal and hope is to live to see it is as a group of national Playmakers coaches who are working from the same mission statement, and the same character playbook, with coaching accountability built in. Add to that a funding mechanism so that some of our coaches' expenses are paid for. Yes, those are big goals, but as Olympic Hockey Coach Herb Brooks once said, "That's why I want to pursue it." What the results of that would be, only our awesome God knows.

One of my many challenges in writing this book (my third coaching book), is I am co-authoring it with a kid/man who has two degrees from Stanford, while I attended San Diego State 40 years ago. That tells me he should feel academically intimidated.

~2~

MEETING "BIGFOOT"

HOW THE PARTNERSHIP BEGAN

I met Harrison Phillips in 2015 through Jordan Richards (one of my Playmakers) when Jordan introduced us during Harrison's freshman year at Stanford. Jordan is a kid (now a man) whom I have watched grow up ever since he played youth football in Folsom, California, my home. My wife, Linda, and I have gone to church with his beautiful parents, Terrance and Sharon Richards. Jordan is one of the smartest, hardest working, selfless young men that I know. Jordan will be the first to tell you that he lives a blessed life, from playing on a state championship high school football team, to the Rose Bowl at Stanford, to earning a Super Bowl ring his rookie year with the New England Patriots. With all of those accomplishments, those are the least impressive things about this man. I remember him in high school coming to our Playmakers events where he would speak to younger at-risk kids about character and serving in our community. I may be getting a little ahead of myself, so let me fill you in on what "Playmakers" is.

Playmakers is a nonprofit that God put me in charge of back in 2009 when I was a volunteer coach in the inner city. I am going to give you the Reader's Digest version (did I just age myself?) of that story. I was coaching in the "war zone" of Sacramento with high school kids where some were living in cars and hotels. We "loosely" began mentoring them to make sure that they survived the weekend.

I attended two funerals that season for kids. We took kids home from practice (like many of us do) and went down streets where the kids told us, "Coach, don't drive down this road without me in the car. It's not safe for you."

The 10-year story of Playmakers now includes having done peer-to-peer mentoring with over 2,000 kids using this game of football as the common gathering point. Today, we work with at-risk kids and kids with special needs in three states—New York, Nebraska, and California. Harrison, Jordan, and I, along with many tremendous Playmakers and volunteers, have a blast working together. Playmakers is either just a coincidence, a freak accident (maybe), or our God has a plan and will use anyone—including a broken, imperfect, approval and performance addict, to help kids while working on my salvation.

I know that I am a volunteer coach, no different than the volunteer coaches across the country. My hope is that as you read this, hear our story, and maybe attend what will be the most unique clinic you will ever attend, you'll see what God can do with YOUR story. My dear friend, Rick Carr, told me several years ago, "Roz, God MUST be involved in Playmakers, because you just are not smart enough to pull this off." Truth from a good friend.

So back to Jordan. While he was at Stanford, he would come each year to our Playmakers dinners and speak to our guests. He was such a humble person, even as a kid. I would tease him in front of 300+ dinner guests by asking him, "Jordan, when you go to the NFL, will you still come to speak at our dinners?"

"Yes", he would humbly reply in front of the audience.

Next, I would ask, "Will I have to pay you a speaker's fee?—Will I have to go through your agent?"

He would humbly say, "No, Coach, you have me in your contacts on the phone."

I was always joking with him about that, but I think it had a purpose—our relationship is personal and transcends football. That reminds me of a point that I will get to later about "your player tree." One more thing about Jordan. When his story is complete, his football accomplishments will be one of his LEAST important accomplishments. As Joe Namath said before Super Bowl III, "I guarantee it."

Jordan was a senior at Stanford at the time and knew that one of his Playmakers responsibilities was to Pay-It-Forward, so he called me and said, "Coach, there is a freshman here, Harrison Phillips from Omaha (where we were doing Playmakers mentoring), and he wants to get involved with Playmakers."

My immediate answer: "Does he have your kind of character?"

"Coach, I Bible study with him and I think he could be a Playmaker." So after the game, Miss Linda and whomever we bring to the game wait for Jordan (last to shower and come out of the locker) to say, "Thank you" and tell him we love him. This is part of the Stanford game ritual.

We live three hours from Stanford. When they play a night game, it ends at about 10 PM. We wait an additional hour for him to shower, get dressed, and come out, so that makes it about 11, and then we start our three-hour drive back home, arriving about 2 AM the next day. Need I say, Miss Linda is a saint!

At this particular game, out walks Jordan with a young, homesick Omaha kid whom I now have nicknamed "Bigfoot"—Harrison Phillips. So the "Harrison Journey" began with me saying, "You are probably connected here at Stanford, but if you just need some home cooking, you are more than welcome to visit us."

I remember him saying, "I don't know anyone here, and I really appreciate it," so we exchanged phone numbers and talked a little about Omaha.

Miss Linda and I had no idea where that would go, and of course, no idea what God had in mind for Harrison, or what a special young man He had put in our path.

GETTING ACQUAINTED

Shortly after the season ended, we sent Harrison a train ticket to Sacramento, so when he had a "free" weekend, he came for his first visit. He got off the train, computer under his arm, to stay with us. Now there is another story here about Tammie and Paul Phillips, two of the best people I now know. Imagine, Bigfoot calling his parents and telling them that "some family" three hours away has invited him to come and just hang out for the weekend. As a parent, I would be asking a ton of why, what do they want, and what's in it for them questions? They were just so grateful, and we have developed a tremendous "Playmakers Family" relationship with them that has included many laughs, cries, victories, draft day, injuries, and experiences that we cherish.

Miss Linda loves telling the story of his first visit when he just slept. He was so grateful to have a bed where he didn't have to hang off the end. At Stanford, athletes truly get few special considerations, including their beds. He was too big for his dorm bed and had to sleep sideways.

I remember one of the first conversations we had. This was with a college football player, trying to earn a starting position, and was obsessed with playing in the NFL. I recall saying, "Almost everyone wants to talk football with you, and we will, but I want to talk with you about your family, your faith, and really important things. Is that okay?" That laid the groundwork for some of the best conversations as the years went by.

Let me tell you what our relationship beyond football looks like. We were in Buffalo his rookie year. The NFL has a program called "My Cleats for My Cause." Bigfoot called me and asked for our Playmakers logo artwork. He says they are going to put our logo on his cleats. He'll wear them for a game and then give them to us to auction off at our dinner. When I didn't hear much about it for a couple of weeks, I asked him, "What about that cleat thing?" He asked if I could come to Buffalo in a couple of weeks because we will get recognized at that game. So off to Buffalo I went for a weekend, which I will tell you more about later. Here is the point of the deeper conversations we have. After the game, about 10 of us are at dinner at one of his favorite Buffalo restaurants, and you can just about imagine the football conversation taking place at the table, and our excitement as the guests of Harrison. As the conversation is flowing with and without him, he taps me on the shoulder and whispers, "I need your advice. What is your opinion on adult baptism?"

Now as crazy and out of place as that might seem, you have no idea how that question speaks of our relationship. The man with two degrees from Stanford, is an NFL player with access to a team Chaplain, and resources miles beyond mine, wants my opinion on a faith-based subject. I felt like a proud Dad, mentor, and friend of one of the most unique and complex men I have ever met. You see, Harrison has the ability to store more information and get more done than any man that I know. This is a man who graduated from Stanford in three and a half years with two degrees and more community service than I have seen done. I am learning from him. He handles things as they come so he can take it off his "to do" plate. Harrison is a machine in what he can accomplish. He is constantly in motion doing and achieving much. I watch him in admiration. He is a ham (I mean that in the best sense), a freak for details and getting things done right. To ask him if he is satisfied with a game, an event, a camp we do, or other things, he will constantly be analyzing how it could have been done better. I learn so much from him each time I am around him.

One of the points I am trying to make is that our relationship was not business-planned out. As a relational coach (which is what I hope you aspire to or have achieved—more on that later), like almost all quality relationships, our relationship was intentional and forged in time. The game of football was just the conduit. I honestly believe, and I have told this to Bigfoot many times, that if he never played another down, he would be like a son to me. I do not make that statement lightly. God has a sense of humor and gave me two beautiful daughters. I have a couple of men whom I refer to as the sons I never had. Harrison is one of them. I will tell you about some of the others when we talk about our Players Tree. Harrison, like Jordan, will NOT be defined by his NFL career. He will achieve and contribute much more when all is said and done. I love Harrison Phillips, and I believe he loves me. Again, let me state, I am a volunteer off-campus coach, like most of you, and I have far more game losses than most of you.

THE BIGGER PICTURE

Let me tell you about one of the areas where Bigfoot is shaping my faith walk. As I have said, I am a performance and approval addict. That has been detrimental in my life, and my good friend and Pastor talks about it regularly. One of the questions that Pastor Mike asked me when we began Playmakers was, "If this is just a small ministry that helps a few kids in Sacramento, will that be good enough for you?" I lied to my Pastor and said, "Of course!!" He and I laugh about that today, but believe me, he is invited into my life "at will" (as are others) to keep a close eye on my ego and motives.

Here is how that plays out in faith. I get to design and head up football camps around the country today. They are for at-risk kids and kids with special needs, and the camps are a blast, to say the least. I am usually the center of the show and get plenty of ego-boosting opportunities at those events. They include media, video, interviews, and me with kids all around me, and I LOVE every minute of it. They are the most physically demanding days that I have. At age 63, I have to admit I'm beyond my prime playing days. But there I am, Coach Roz, center stage, with all the "atta boys" most humans can have.

However, when you do those camps in Buffalo and Omaha, where Harrison can win the Mayor's election right now, I am NOT the center of the show. Bigfoot is, and he deserves it. The problem is, that hurts just a bit and my ego can get in the way. Actually, I think that is where God wants me, behind Harrison and just being a good support system to him. That is a faith growth point for me, and Harrison was instrumental in that. You see, God will only trust you in the bigger things when you can handle the little things. (Matthew 25:21)

Getting back to "My Cause for My Cleats," I showed up in Buffalo. Prior to the event, I got to talk with Bills' Executive, Preston Teague, who brought up all Harrison is doing for local charity in Buffalo HIS ROOKIE SEASON, how the Bills love his work, and that they have to be careful that he paces his charity activities so he doesn't hit the rookie wall.

When I told Preston what we're doing for free for at-risk kids and kids with special needs through our Buffalo Camp the coming Spring, he loved it. When Preston asked where we plan to do the camp, I told him we hadn't found a school yet, so he "suggests" that we do it at the Bills facility. Are you kidding me?? A Playmakers Character Football Camp at an NFL stadium? And FOR FREE???

Now think back to what my buddy in Sac said to me—"Roz, God MUST be involved in Playmakers because you just are not smart enough to pull this off." Coaches, you know that coaching is redundant, so I am going to continue to make redundant statements. I am just a volunteer coach, like most of you who are relational coaches, and I'm getting more blessings than I deserve. Preston said to me later, "Do you have any idea how many organizations want to do their camps here that we say 'no' to?"

WHY THE BILLS' STADIUM?

Harrison has been part of our Playmakers Camps for five years. When he was drafted, he asked us to do a camp in Buffalo where he plays, and that we continue to do one in Omaha, where he is from. It may surprise you that my philosophy on football camps is that I don't think the world needs one more football camp. The problem that I have with football camps is that (usually a kid/family) pays $100 plus to get a t-shirt, run a few drills, and go home while the host pockets some spending cash. That is fine, it's just not what Playmakers is about. Now Harrison knows it takes about $10,000 to cover the cost of our camps, and we do four of them per summer. He also told me there is one in Lincoln, NE, that draws almost 1,000 kids. I know that is what he has in mind, as Bigfoot thinks big on things like this.

So I mustered up the best sales presentation that I could and said to Bigfoot, "Harrison, there are so many regular football camps, what if we did one that leaves an indelible mark on all who participate? One for kids with special needs who may NEVER play football, as well as kids who cannot afford to go to a camp at all?" At first, I was not too sure what he thought of that, because he had a camp in Lincoln in the back of his head and I was the only one who knew what my idea was going to look like, but he appeased me and said okay. That's how I remember the conversation. Here is where I raised the price of poker when I said, "I think we can do something that is not being done, and that we can do the best camp in the country." Now we have something that is worthy of doing, and doing well, which is the only way that we will do it.

I remember Harrison saying something about doing a regular camp, too, which just confirmed to me that he was not yet clear on what exactly we were going to do. Here is the funny thing about that. I wasn't sure what we were going to do either. I had not done a special needs camp yet and had no clue what that looked like. All I knew at this point was, Harrison agreed to do one and if it did not go well, my approval, performance, and pride would take a huge hit. Would my creditability with Harrison go out the window? Could our relationship stand that? After all, he was now in the NFL, had many more resources than I did, and did not need me or Playmakers to do summer camps.

Again, this is where this man of God, Harrison, teaches me much. To think that our relationship is based on what I just laid out, he would laugh, because his faith runs deep. He is a man of character and that just is not how he rolls. I also think that our character is shaped by situations like what we're proposing to do, where you don't know the outcome, and must trust God.

How can you put that lesson into your coaching model? Here are several ways:

Coach a position that is not your usual coaching position.
Speak to the kids on a character-based subject.
Tell the kids where YOU made a mistake.
Ask for forgiveness.
Show empathy, not your toughness.
Look a player in the eye and tell him, I LOVE YOU.
Ask a kid to imitate you. It can be pretty revealing.
We will talk about all of these and more in our coaches' clinic.

Our clinics look much like our camps. They can be transformative and life changing. If you are coming to our clinics to get "coached up" on cover two, inside screen, or a new play, don't come to ours, because our clinics are lessons in how to change a kid's life for the better. Our clinics are about teaching parents their role. They are about how you grow relationships like Harrison and I have developed. If that is what you're willing to take a look at, we can't wait to meet you. We can't wait to hear your stories about how you are using this great game to change the world.

"YOU'RE JUST THE FIRE HYDRANT AT THE DOG SHOW"

Harrison's and my conversations are bathed in sarcasm and mixed with love. Believe me, I know the danger of sarcasm and where it fits in our Bible. It can be a dangerous and slippery slope. That's not an excuse, but my lifetime in athletics is filled with athletes telling each other that they are not as good as they are. So one day we were watching Bigfoot play, and my wife wanted to know where exactly he was on the field. I started my explanation at the quarterback.

(Most casual fans know where the quarterback is.) She knew that, and I then showed her (and she knew) where the center was, the guy who hiked the ball to the quarterback. From there we moved to the other side of the ball, and we found the nose tackle (one of Harrison's positions). She said, "Wow, there is a big pile of players around him."

I agreed with her and said, "He is kind of like the fire hydrant at the dog show." She laughed until soda came out of her nose. Later, I told Bigfoot my explanation of his position and he liked it. Since then, I have heard him use that description in sound bites and interviews, and I suggested I should receive royalties when he uses it. He has not yet agreed to that.

That brings me to our financial relationship, and while that is a personal matter, I mention it here to be as transparent as possible, and to give you a glimpse both into Harrison's heart and our relationship. Harrison is one of the most generous young men I have met. You can only imagine how many people have their hands out wanting a donation from people like Harrison, although there are not many like Harrison. My goal in his and my relationship with him is that he NEVER has to get into his wallet for what Playmakers is doing with kids. I wish I could tell you that is where we are, but his heart is too big for my personal desire. The dollar amount is not important, but let's just say, I owe him more than I will ever be able to repay. Along that line, where athletes at Harrison's elite level navigate, there is such a misconception about what they earn, actually net, and what their financial life looks like. I will tell you here (unless Bigfoot edits it out) that he lives a modest, practical lifestyle that I am so proud of.

~3~

"IT'S DIFFERENT"

LOVE YA, MAN!

I hate that statement, and here is why. Harrison is one of several men (and boys) that I tell regularly, "I love you." Yes, man to man, I look him in the eye, usually when we're saying goodbye, and I tell him, "I love you." He always tells me that he loves me. Remember that we're not related (except in Christ), not husband and wife, father and son. We're just two men whom God brought together through a great game.

Now understand that I work, coach, and mentor kids who come from broken homes and live in situations that you would have trouble getting your mind around. Some of "my kids" come from places where they may not have heard "I love you" from a father, or a man they can trust, in a LONG TIME. Some, maybe never. That breaks my heart in ways that I cannot write, but it is the truth. I have sat in faith-based men's groups and witnessed men in tears with a lifetime of regrets, and part of their story is not knowing that their earthly father loves them unconditionally. There are libraries of faith-based and secular books on this subject. The point is, I believe my job as a coach is to create as many long-lasting relationships with kids where saying "I love you" is possible. There will be more on this when we encourage you, as a coach and man of character, to write your eulogy while you're still here.

I hope I don't need to point out here that I mean "I love you" in the most wholesome, character-based, safe way as is humanly possible. Let me give you one of many Playmakers examples here. This story combines several memories and learnings at the same time. I have a kid, now a man, whose dad left his mom while he was young. This created a mistrust between him and his father that was never healed because, during this period of his life, his dad died of cancer. You can imagine the hurricane in this kid's formative years. As he and I developed a relationship over his teens and beyond, I had no idea what it meant (or didn't mean) when I looked him in the eye and told him, "I love you." I don't say, "love ya, man." I wanted him to know, in his soul, that I really do love him. I want him to know that he is loved by a man whom he can trust. How is that going to shape him when he is married and has a son? I am not yet sure, but I am going to do the best I can, AS A FORMER COACH OF HIS, to convince him that I love him. When he speaks at my funeral, I pray that my telling him "I love you" regularly, made a difference. It certainly did for me.

Harrison gets no different treatment than the kid I just told you about. Harrison comes from a tremendous Dad and Mom, Paul and Tammie. He has been raised right, by two good people who taught him values that any father would be proud of. How does Paul feel about my saying that? I will ask him when he reads this, but my guess is he is okay with that.

While I'm on this subject, I tell Harrison how proud I am of him. Occasionally, I will text him, "Do you get tired of me telling you how proud I am of you?" His answer is always the same up until now — "Nope." It does seem kind of silly to tell a man with all his accomplishments on and off the field how proud I am of him. He is pretty sure of all he has done. He does not need that from me, but he is going to hear it as long as I am around. So what am I so proud of?

Here are just a few reasons:
- The day after he tore up his knee (season-ending injury), he is at the kids' hospital, visiting kids.
- He seeks out the area of the hospital where KIDS ARE NOT VISITED REGULARLY for reasons that most of us don't think of. He spends time with kids where the cameras don't go.
- Harrison was frustrated when he played in the Shrine Game because he did not get enough time with the kids at the Shrine Hospital.
- His picture is hanging at a kids' agency in Buffalo where he spends time regularly.
- He lets kids hang on him, drool on him, poke at him, and use his body as a jungle gym when what he needs is healing.
- Seeing his emotions bring him to tears for the lost, broken, and forgotten.
- Texting kids 3,000 miles away because he has given them his personal cell to contact him when they want to.

That is just the short list. There is much more, but I think you get the idea and a glimpse of what makes this man special. As I have said many times, the NFL will not be Harrison's most significant contribution when he is all done.

KIDS WITH SPECIAL NEEDS

Currently, we work with at-risk kids and kids with special needs. I am still not sure what the differences are between the two. Years ago, when we were working with at-risk kids in our after school program, we were certainly aware that some of those kids had physical challenges. In addition to that, we were aware that some of them had social challenges as well, including anger issues and other behavioral problems. We just lumped them all together and treated them all like Playmakers kids.

As my relationship with Harrison increased, he introduced me to a tremendous organization in Buffalo called Bornhava, which is a school that specializes in kids with special needs, particularly ones with Down syndrome. That is where I met a wonderful woman by the name of Debbie Cavers. Between Debbie, Harrison, and this tremendous school, my sensitivity to these has kids increased significantly.

In the year that I have known Debbie, she has fallen in love with Playmakers, and we have fallen in love with her. Debbie has formed a board of directors for Playmakers in Buffalo and now serves as our regional director—just another piece of the Playmakers puzzle that I had no idea was going to happen. Through this relationship and our mutual love for kids and sports, it just naturally occurred. Debbie took Playmakers' core principles to a city 3,000 miles away and is just running with it. Debbie's efforts are reaching new kids and new families, and new Playmakers relationships are developing.

One of the first things that happened in Buffalo was meeting this unbelievable kid named Blake. Blake has Down syndrome. He also has a heart that will melt you. As I saw how much he loved sports, he and I immediately gravitated toward one another. Blake played on the JV football team when I met him. He loves having the uniform and being part of the game. As our relationship deepened, Blake gave me the idea of developing a kids' board of directors so he and other kids could have input as to the direction of Playmakers. Blake currently sits on that board.

As I have already mentioned, we do various football and sports camps around the country. I've done one of my annual camps for 15 years with Tim Brown. Tim is in the NFL Hall of Fame, is a former Heisman Trophy winner, and a tremendous man of faith. We introduced kids with special needs to Tim at my camp a year ago, and he absolutely loved it. As we're preparing for this year's camp, we are expanding the number of these kids who will participate in our camps.

Our camp in Omaha was filled with kids with special needs. It was there that we really began to expand what we could do with them by simply having fun while stretching their sports capabilities. The biggest thing that we learned was to treat them no differently than any other kid in camp. All of those kids were able to participate in all of the activities at their own levels. That seemed good enough. What I was not expecting was the impact it was having on the parents. Those parents, for a limited period of time, did not have to supervise or monitor their child's activities. They turned that over to us. They trusted us, and allowed us to experiment and just have fun.

It was in Omaha that I first met Ande. Ande is a beautiful young woman who is in a wheelchair. This was the first person we have had in our camps who was in a wheelchair, and I honestly did not know what that was going to look like. One of the things we do when our camps begin is have an all-participants dance. It's that silly dance people sometimes do at weddings that includes stomping your feet and spinning in circles, somewhat like a line dance. I can't tell you how much fun I had with Ande. It was the first time that I danced with someone who was in a wheelchair, and it grew my heart. I have no idea how many times Ande has danced, but I do know that she danced once at a Playmakers camp.

Harrison also introduced me to Unified Basketball. I believe it was founded by Special Olympics, and it is tremendous. It allows kids with special needs to play basketball with the assistance of another young person who does not have those special needs. Imagine the diversity and understanding that develops when two of those kids are working together playing a game. I saw this first in Buffalo, and it fascinated me. When I came back to California and met with the Special Olympics representative in Sacramento, he said that type of basketball does not exist in Sacramento. That's all I needed to hear. We organized the first game, and the outcome was amazing. We had 15 kids with special needs participating in basketball with one of the local high school's freshman football teams assisting them. The outcome was amazing. One set of parents came to us and said it was the first time their child had ever participated in basketball with someone other than themselves. While that was hard for me to believe, I have no reason to doubt it. All I know is we facilitated something extremely easy to do and, for that child, it was a first experience. Mission accomplished!

That leads us to our second basketball game for kids with special needs, which we will be doing in the next 60 days. An additional spinoff of that idea is that these kids will now get to participate during halftime at a college basketball game. What an experience that will be—not only for the participants but for everyone who will get to watch that event!

Gang, I am no more or less talented than anyone reading this book. This is just what developing a relationship with someone like Harrison can lead to. When those relationships are forged, through football, look at what can happen. Look at what God can do. See how He can use us and this great game to help an unlimited number of kids and families.

We now have a core of volunteers who are developing a special needs Unified Basketball League. That means these kids and families will get to experience this on a regular basis. After basketball, when the weather gets good, we can add outdoor sports. If this idea comes to fruition, we may have year-round sports activities for these kids. This is just part of our vision.

Let's take a look at what kids with special needs require in order to play outdoor sports. Oftentimes, they need a field that can accommodate their challenges. In Sacramento we have something called Independence Field. It was developed by a friend of mine who pulled resources together and built a field that is ADA compliant for kids in wheelchairs and/or who have other disabilities. I wish you could see what that looks like. I'm talking about a fair playing field that allows kids, who otherwise could not play, get to play and have a blast outdoors. As I have looked at the other cities where we presently have influence (Buffalo and Omaha), I have not found where a field like that exists. We are in the beginning stages of figuring out what it would look like to develop more of those fields. The cost to do that is going to be approximately two million dollars! Yes, I said $2,000,000.

That is a large dollar amount for this volunteer coach. I am excited to think about what possibilities exist and who might get involved in a project such as this. In addition to kids with special needs, this field could serve Wounded Warriors and their rehabilitation. The possibilities just keep getting bigger and bigger.

For projects of this size to happen, I believe we must partner with other agencies with similar goals and objectives. This means agencies like Special Olympics, Wounded Warriors, and others. You and I are volunteer football coaches. What I have just outlined are things we all have access to where we live. All of us can connect with civic groups. All of us can connect with our churches. All of us can seek out special needs agencies, including Special Olympics. It's just a matter of including that into your coaching mission statement because you want to use football for the greater good of the community and the kids. This is coaching that is thinking outside the box. Imagine what it would look like if we got together for clinics where we could brainstorm and work together, seeking out new ideas, new possibilities, and new ways to help kids. That is why I want to coach, and that's what Harrison is all about, too.

Where is faith in all of that? As I write about a $2,000,000 field, that is a resource challenge for me. For someone else who is reading this, or perhaps for someone you know, that may be an easy task. Some coach (or Harrison-type person) knows how to write grants for these kids. Some coach knows someone who can assist with goals like these. This morning I sat down at 7 AM with one of my board members and reviewed what we have going. It looks like this:

- Kids with special needs sports league
- Organizing FREE youth tackle football for 100 kids and families in Sacramento
- Three-year plan for a Playmakers field for kids with special needs
- Sac State Football Players leaders organization (ten will be mentoring our kids)
- Stanford Football Players leaders organization (two right now)

- Trip for Playmakers kids to go to Legoland
- Fundraising and grant writing

He asked practical questions that sometimes get in my way. I'm much better at dreaming big, casting a vision, and recruiting. His advice was simple—stay focused. Somewhere in all this is the fundraising that will include how we help volunteer coaches get paid for some of their expenses. We'll discuss that plan at our clinics.

YOUR COACHING TREE

I am so proud of mine, and I hope you will indulge me for a moment. I know many of you have coached longer than my 10 years and your tree may be bigger (I hope it is). One of the exercises at our clinics is to write out your players' tree. Here is an outline of mine:

- Three current Pastors
  - Two senior Pastors
  - One Youth Pastor
- One Chief Petty Officer
- Multiple career military men (all branches)
- The Director of the International Justice Mission in Washington, DC, who leads a global organization that breaks up child pornography rings
- One high school graduate (barely) who has slept on our sofa MANY times. Today, he drives a million-dollar truck cross country for a living to care for his three children and his mom. He survived "the streets" funerals of friends and family. Lost his wife to meth. He calls me at random times and says, "I love you, Coach." He is the one who told me, when I was taking him home from practice, not to drive down the street he lived on without him, day or night. He has not quit, given up, left his family, or been selfish about his own wants and what the street offers. He is a different color than I am. He has taught me much about race, and more.
- Several husbands, and now dads

Coaches, my prayer is that these kids (they're all kids, to me) who have been part of our "family" will have something to say at my funeral and then will help carry me home.

YOUR EULOGY

Let's talk about this part of our clinic. It is the exercise of writing your eulogy. I am in a men's Saturday morning 7 AM group of faith-based guys that I have been with for over 10 years. We're a group of men whom I have grown to love, as we've done life together for a long time. We have survived a lot of things together—including marriages, divorces, kids, and all that goes with that, cancer—survival and non-survival (I am one of the survivors). Sometimes we enter into discussions of how we want our final years to look like. How do we FINISH WELL? I want to finish well. I want to "game plan" what the end of this game looks like. What does that mean for me, and how do I want to be remembered? I am just opening up a topic that is healthy to look into—designing, not settling, for where we are in life. As a volunteer coach, this is huge for me, as the kids around me are such a major part of how I'll finish well. I believe that may be the case for you as well. Come to our clinic and let's work through it together, and then we'll spread the word.

You may find it odd that I speak and write about my eulogy. It inspires me to think it through. It gives me the opportunity to leave nothing on the table. Don't get me wrong. I have also written a 30-year plan, and I am 63, I think. As someone whose name I can't remember said, "When my participation in the game of life ends, I don't want to be caught asking for 'extra innings.'"

Think about this for a minute. If you are a "head coach" of any average team, you probably have an influence with about 20-40 kids plus their families. That could be up to 60 people. If you're a position coach, maybe 10 kids and families. The point is, we influence a bunch of people. I believe that we are "pastors" in our community, and our church or congregation is our team. We have the structure in place to affect more people than you can get your arms around. Imagine your voice on these subjects to young people in the following areas of life, for life:

- Empathy
- Character
- Treatment of women
- Serving others
- Commitment to community
- Education
- Respect

I could go on and on. My Pastor of a church of nearly 1,000 is also a freshman football coach. He is one of the most dynamic, spot-on influential persons I know. Ask him if he has more community impact leading our church or as the coach of a freshman football team. He will tell you, hands down, as a football coach.

COACHING FOOTBALL

About 25 years ago, a D1 college football coach by the name of Bill McCartney founded Promise Keepers, a faith-based organization that impacted hundreds of thousands of men around the world. Led by a coach, it has brought men to better character-based, wife-honoring, Christ-like behavior. I admit I am biased, as it was Promise Keepers that changed my life, forever. Like anything that has world impact, including the life of Christ, Promise Keepers has its doubters and was very controversial, but its effect has been long-lasting and positive.

So here is a vision. What would it look like if there were prepared, trained coaches—first in our city, then around the country—who are on the same mission with the same game plan and playbook? We coaches would prepare motivated kids with the same consistency. But how are the kids motivated, you ask?

Through incentives:

We can create teams and leagues that are of little or no financial expense to the families. This does not mean free, with no commitment. It means that the kids' and families' tuition and fees are clearly outlined and agreed upon.

Through behavior:

Kids who want to play on these teams MUST be cleared by someone of authority. This could be their teachers. Imagine a teacher with a student who is a pain in their classroom. The kid plays youth football and that is the most important thing going on in this kid's social life. The kid knows that Coach's phone number is in their teacher's phone. If the kid is to play on Saturday, the teacher's input is considered in that decision. The teacher now has leverage (power) in how that kid behaves in the classroom. Yes, that is "old school," and would need the participation of the parent, as well. I can't tell you how much respect you will gain from that teacher. You have formed a team that includes more people of character. You have elevated academics into the equation. You are reinforcing Playmakers' four core values of Academics, Family, Serving Others, and Winning with Honor into the sports and social equation. Here are some of the questions that you might be asking as a coach at this point:

1. Is that really my role as a volunteer youth coach?
   I believe that it is if you want a lifelong impact on kids by creating servant leaders for future generations.
2. Isn't that a lot of work?
   Do I need to answer that? If it weren't, everyone would be doing it.

3. Will the parents appreciate it?
   Hopefully, but parents are broken, and we cannot guarantee that either they—or the kids—will understand it at the time. I have had many kids (and parents) seek me out later and say, "Thank you," and more.
4. Will the teachers participate?
   Most that I have established a relationship with do participate and do appreciate the effort.
5. Will the kid respond in a positive manner?
   Some will, and some won't.

ARE YOU GIVING YOUR BEST EFFORT?

This has been one of the fairest, get to the point questions that I ask kids today. Most kids have been gifted with different abilities and talents in the classroom, yet today not all kids have the same opportunity in the classroom. I have coached two kids who were twins who lived in a one-bedroom apartment with eight family members, including a baby. The two kids were often late to school because they had to get dressed in the dark so as not to wake the baby. I have had kids who are hungry and not properly nourished. How can we believe that those kids can compete academically with others? All I want from those kids is their best effort. I think that is all you can ask. When I go meet with a player and his teacher and the three of us talk, I begin by asking his teacher, "Is my player giving you his best effort?" You can predict what the answer usually is.

You may be asking, "What do you do if he has six teachers?" You can accomplish the same by asking his parents the same question. You will begin by becoming a relational coach who holds kids accountable at levels not familiar to most kids or their parents. If you are at the youth level, you are preparing kids and families so the high school coach's job will be easier. If you are a high school coach, you are teaching the kid accountability. You are investing in his future.

In our country, two out of five kids are living in a home without their biological father. In the areas where I coach, the statistic is much higher. One-third of these kids are being raised by a single mom. If we gain trust in those broken families, we can change the trajectory of a child, and their family, too. The question is, will you, coach, accept the challenge and learn how to do it? Our prayer is that you will. Harrison and I would like to be a part of that process.

~4~

THE FUTURE

WE HAVE A LONG WAY TO GO

Coaches could be the catalyst of a systemic change across our county. We could use the most effective laboratory invented (the field of play) to make life changes in our society. We could be treating each other better, respectfully. We could be developing character-based, empathic, understanding leaders who would put our society in a better place.

We have a tremendous amount of house cleaning to do first. This is not the pretty part, nor is it fun to talk about. These challenges are some of the reasons that I want to stick my finger down my throat when it comes to youth sports, beginning with the one that I love, football. Clearly understand that I have not found a sport immune to the contamination of what is happening. The exercise that I am going to ask you to do next is based on fact, according to Google, not my opinion.

Google the following:
- Embezzlement in youth sports (any city you choose)
- Hazing in sports (including youth sports)
- Bullying in sports
- Sexual exploitation

- Social media and more
- Gambling in youth sports
- Bad parent behavior in youth sports
- Referee abuse
- Youth steroids

Stand in this for just a minute and resist the urge to dismiss this due to region, socioeconomic differences, coach screening, and more. Your rationalizations just will not hold up. Some of these travesties involve kids, other people, parents, and in some cases, both.

Now layer on top of that, travel ball, personal trainers, and year-round, one-sport families. It just goes on and on. You might be thinking it is one thing to just get on my soapbox and shout at the moon, but it is quite another to offer some suggestions, which we do, but they are not just suggestions. They are principles that we've implemented that seem to make sense. They just require a willingness to look at things differently.

For me, it began with becoming a disciple of a man whose story I read and then had the privilege to meet several years ago, Joe Ehrmann. My intersection with Joe came at a time when I was looking for the right model for mentoring/coaching, as well as faith-based self-help. I do not think that meeting Joe was a coincidence. Like most good coaches will admit, there is not much new in coaching. Things just have been recycled and repackaged. Little of my writings or clinics are "original" ideas. They are just suggestions that have been applied, tweaked, and repackaged.

The single most important book in coaching I have ever read was about Joe's story in "Season of Life" by Jeffrey Marx. It changed and shaped my coaching and mentoring philosophy considerably.

Not only is this a tremendous book about coaching, it's a book about understanding the relationships between boys and their fathers. It also is a lesson in the subject of true masculinity, a subject that I find very few men are willing to discuss or have a healthy understanding of.

Go to any coaching clinic today to experience my point. I had the privilege a few years ago of hearing De La Salle's legendary high school coach, Rob Ladouceur, speak on offense line blocking. He was tremendous in telling his audience his secrets, such as:

> They use a "flipper technique" popular 30 years ago, but many believe outdated today. He explained why it works for them, with today's game.

> The time they spend on the sled that other teams don't.

There was nothing new in Coach Ladouceur's teaching, just how they are committed to what they do, and how much time they spend on those basics.

BUILDING A SEASON

Here are a few of the items that we address in our clinics. I can promise you that some coaches have never heard of these, yet they are what makes you an "uncommon man" and a Playmakers Coach.

MISSION STATEMENT (TEAM OR POSITION)

Start your season by creating a mission statement for your team or (at the least) your position. A crafted mission statement will put you into the top percentage of coaches. Many coaches and their programs will have one, and many will not. If you are going to be a Playmakers coach, with people who care about you and your program, showing them on paper what you are about will greatly impress them.

PERSONAL MISSION STATEMENT

A few years ago, I was watching a special on one of my childhood heroes, Merlin Olsen. It was about the original "Fearsome Foursome" and their lifelong bond during, and more importantly, after football.

Merlin was a special man in so many ways. Before cancer took his life, he had crafted a PERSONAL MISSION STATEMENT. You read that right—not a corporate statement, but a personal one. It was a written declaration of how he chose to live his life. It has inspired me to write one of my own. I have met very few people who are so intentional about their life that they would put their life's mission on paper for others to see. His lesson inspired me to do the same. While it is not nearly as impressive as Merlin's, I have begun the process, and continue to craft it even today.

SHORTER PRACTICE

In one of Tony Dungy's books, he said he has never coached a game that has taken more than three days to prepare for. That struck me, so we now have worked that philosophy into our Playmakers model. I have seen far too many youth practices drag on for over two hours due to wasted time. An organized practice plan will move things along and allow you to get to far more important things. A large part of football is about time management. It is so much fun to watch a well-run module practice and see how the individual pieces come together with little or no wasted time. I never get tired of watching it.

Most of us who coach football believe it may be the greatest game that God invented. There is beauty in so many parts. I particularly care about the details of the game. That includes the uniform, which closely resembles battle armor. For me it begins with the socks. I tell our kids that you can wear ANY color socks you want but ONLY if they are WHITE WITH NOTHING MORE ON THEM. Pink, tie-dye socks, or kids insisting that they have the manufacturer's logo just is not important. Besides, some kids cannot afford those designer labels.

I bet you can guess where I am on the whole idea of stickers on your helmet. We will discuss in our clinic what a sticker for a touchdown says about the values of the team. I realize that you can have team stickers, but don't let that take away from the game and the beauty of the uniform. If you really think stickers are important, then how about putting stickers on the helmet for a 3.0 GPA or community service? Those are sticker-worthy.

Cancer month. I am a cancer survivor, so I do get a qualified opinion on this. I just believe there are ways your team can make a stand for cancer without wearing pink socks. My players always wear white socks and are in uniform.

Back to building a season. Your parent meetings (particularly the first ones) should be laid out so there is a clear vision of where you are taking the team and their family. That includes:

- Team mission statement
- Personal mission statement
- Grade and conduct checks
- Parent contract
- Clear problem-solving communication path
- If you are late to practice
- If you miss practice
- Parents at practice, do's and don'ts

When a parent/observer sees a Playmakers practice, here is what they will see:
- A head coach in coaching attire with a whistle around his neck
- Assistant coaches in coaching attire (no street clothes)
- Coaches with whistles and clipboards
- Kids having fun (usually)
- Coaches saying
  - I love you
  - I am sorry
  - I was wrong
  - Are you having fun?
  - Tell me about your day at school

WHAT YOU WILL NOT SEE (OR HEAR)

- Coaches yelling at kids
- Foul language—NEVER an "F-bomb"
- Kids being grabbed or manhandled
- Parents on the practice field
- Kids standing around in uniform "watching" practice
- Bullying
- Incorrect tackling drills
- Kids practicing who were not in school

BEGINNING YOUR PRACTICE

AGENDA

As practice begins, get the kids together and CLEARLY lay out the agenda for the entire practice. Don't overcomplicate it. "Team, here is what we're going to do today, and we're going to go fast, okay?"

- When warming up, have the kids come onto the field fast
- Rugby tackling (everyone will get at least 20 GOOD tackles)
  - Knees
  - ½ speed
  - ¾ speed (Sideline)
- Line will go with Coach (insert name) for Blocking EDD's (Every Day Drills) and Insert Jet Sweep
- Receivers will do "Bad Balls" (100 catches)

You show me a youth practice where 10-year-olds are catching 100 balls the first 20 minutes of practice. Also, 20 good form Rugby tackles done the first 20 minutes of practice.

This is a sample of setting the E.I.A. (Expectations, Incentives, Agenda)

EXPECTATIONS

"Kids, we expect you to go hard and fast. You must pay attention, ask good questions, and listen well. Does that sound okay?" (Get agreement)

INCENTIVES

"If we go fast, pay attention, and get it done, we will take off the shoulder pads and helmets later on. (Would you like that?) Finally, if we RUN to formation, finish the play and……. etc, that will be our conditioning. No lap running or wind sprints. (Would you like that?)"

What we're doing here is building leverage. To some degree, we're bargaining for a good practice. Does it work? Some days better than others, no different than all football practices. These kids respond to incentives, positive encouragement, and praise, no different than we adults do at work.

WHERE IS IT FUN?

How are you, as a coach, making this game fun? Tell me where the fun is in running wind sprints? Tell me where the fun is in running a kid around the field as a coach yells at him? Tell me where you are teaching an overweight kid how to love the game by making him a lineman, and he NEVER touches the ball? Or by laying two kids on their backs and having them Billy Goat head-on into one another to see who is the toughest?

Go watch a well-run high school practice, a college practice, or the NFL channel and you NEVER see what I have just described. If you really dig down on why kids are running laps or why there is too much full-contact scrimmaging, it is because the coach has run out of coaching techniques. Too often coaches run kids because they are acting out at practice with no clue about what they have endured at home and in school.

Kids get disciplined for not knowing their plays when in almost all instances, the coach has too many plays to begin with. Ask yourself this question: "What are you going to do today and at practice that makes that overweight, non-athlete, marginally interested kid WANT to be at your practice?" This is the kid who is trying to figure out his masculinity, who may be being told that he "must toughen up" and play football because his dad did. He may be coming home from practice with some male influence, teaching him that if he is going to be a "man," he must learn how to hit AND LOVE IT. I could go on for pages here, but my suggestion is that you read "Season of Life" by Jeffrey Marx. You will learn a lifetime about coaching, mentoring, and false masculinity.

In most instances today, you will see men "teaching" the game, teaching the techniques with very little scrimmage time. If you are going to coach, you MUST get current about what your coaching philosophy is. Are you willing to change? I have met many coaches who say, "I have five years coaching experience." That very well may be, but it's also possible that they do not have five years of experience. They have one year, five times, and there is a difference.

My good friend and former teammate, Phil DuBois, has spent his adult life studying, staying current, and coaching speed and body movement. He will amaze you on what is and isn't necessary in stretching and teaching kids to move, while loving sports. It makes him ashamed of our game when he sees kids running laps, wind sprints, and wasting valuable teaching time. He works at our clinics and loves working with coaches who want to learn.

Phil and I first met in 1978 while playing at San Diego State. We're Aztecs and that was our first shared experience. Phil was a running back from Southern California and a tremendous all-around athlete. He was drafted to play pro baseball and chose to play football. That led to him having a career with the Washington Redskins, and later in the USFL. Phil is one of the humblest men that I know. He's going to be ticked that I mentioned that he played for the Washington Redskins when he reads this.

Phil and I got re-acquainted about 30 years later through a mutual Aztec, Dave Katzenmeyer. It's not a coincidence how Dave brought us together. Dave is another man of faith whom I respect a great deal. Phil was living on the East Coast, and through our re-connection, I eventually went out to visit him. Phil had been coaching high school football and mentoring, so we've had a great deal in common as adults (if you can call either of us adults). When he and I are together, I will tell people that I tutored him in college, and he copied my papers. He "really" likes that. The truth is Phil is one of the most academic men I know. He loves to learn and graduated with a degree in English. He is an avid reader and lifelong learner, and is presently writing his book.

Over the years, Phil has become a tremendous student of mentoring kids, as well as training athletes at a high level. Phil loves just working with kids and helping them understand how their body moves. He also uses the game to deepen relationships. Phil is one of the guys that I agree with when he says that a lot of kids do not need to play football, but should be exploring other areas where they're gifted. Our job is to help kids explore what those gifts are. That could include music, art, and other activities where relationships can be developed.

Phil just knows how to mentor and work with kids in unique ways. He uses his skills and the game to its best use. Phil endured an incredible amount of disabilities through his football career. As a professional football player, he has gone from running back to playing tight end in the NFL. His body is the result of a series of collisions that have taken their toll. He is one of the most physically and mentally tough men that I know. In addition to the physical challenges that he has, he has endured losses in his family that would crush most people, but he just continues to move on. I admire him in so many ways.

So as you can see, this book has little to do with the nuts and bolts of coaching and more about relationships and using this game for its highest purpose.

MORE RELATIONSHIPS THROUGH FOOTBALL

After my senior year at San Diego State, I had my second Tommy John surgery and rehabbed my arm as best I could. The problem that I had was that my hand would go numb, so I could not feel the ball in my hand. That is pretty inconvenient for a quarterback. To compound the problem, I began to change my throwing motion because my arm hurt. The result of that was a tear in my rotator cuff. If your shoulder hurts due to a torn rotator cuff and your hand going numb don't count, I was ready to go.

My agent got me a tryout with the Raiders as a punter. Each summer, they will bring in "extra" players for a variety of reasons. None the less, I was getting a tryout with the Oakland Raiders. If you are as old as I am, you may remember that the Raiders already had a punter—his name is Ray Guy. Ray is arguably one of the greatest punters in the history of the NFL. That was okay, I could beat him out. NOT!

I punted okay during the tryout, but nothing really caught their attention. At the end of the tryout, one of the evaluators said, "You were a quarterback, too. Would you like to throw while you are here?" It seemed like a good idea, so I did. One of the tests they gave quarterbacks was having you stand flat-footed and throw the ball, all arm, to test arm strength and, in all honesty, I had a pretty strong arm. I could throw the ball 70 yards (which is a decent throw), but I could stand flat-footed and throw it 55 yards. Besides that, I threw well that day and was signed as a free agent.

It was there that I met David Humm, who would come to be one of my heroes. Hummer took me under his wing and showed me how to get around training camp. Hummer was from Las Vegas, went to the University of Nebraska, and is still a legend there to this day. For some reason or another, David liked me. One of the first pieces of advice David gave me was, "Look, you're a rookie. You're going to get cut. If you try to stay out of everybody's way and be silent, you'll get cut quicker, or you can catch somebody's eye by being a little bit entertaining, and they'll keep you around a bit longer."

Without getting into too much detail, let's just say I did exactly what Hummer told me to do. Speaking in general terms, I found every bit of mischief I could get into while in training camp, but it was over that six-week period that Hummer and I forged a friendship that would last for a lifetime.

Hummer was one of the most amazing men I have ever met. Sadly, Hummer left us too soon due to multiple sclerosis. It was through David that I was introduced to a woman who lives in Omaha, NE, and her name is Donna Miesbach. Donna has played such an important role in my life and has mentored me in so many ways. I admire this woman in ways that bring me to tears just trying to write about her. The first word that I would use to describe Donna is ELEGANT. She is one of the most elegant women I know. She has an external beauty that is like a portrait. God spent an afternoon water-coloring, and painted Donna. Do you get that Donna is beautiful? It only begins there. Donna is one of the smartest people I know. Donna is well-read, a writer, a life coach, a coach of yoga, and more. More than anyone else, Donna has shown me that ALL of our lives are a story worth writing about. I love Donna Miesbach. Donna "claims" to be retired, but I can't begin to keep up with her schedule.

Donna has been with me on the sidelines when I am coaching. She has orchestrated and worked summer football camps with me, and been on many corporate appointments and speaking engagements. Donna and I sat in Dr. Tom Osborne's office when we met him before watching the Nebraska Spring Game. Donna and I have stood on top of Hoover Dam, and we have laughed and cried together, all through football. It was Donna who gave me the confidence to write two coaching books. Donna is the co-author. We are now writing our third book together. By the way, Donna is 85 years young. She inspires me. She will be one of the speakers at my funeral.

One of the many beautiful things about Donna's and my relationship is that we are complete opposites. Her soul is as calm as a lake with no wind. Mine is a hurricane, most days. She has the patience of Job (I keep putting in Biblical people) even though I need everything done in 90 days. Donna finds the beauty in most anything, whereas I'm only interested in what benefits me in the moment. When I was diagnosed with the same cancer that took Farrah Faucet (I just aged myself), she prayed for me and held me high. She is a tremendous woman of faith. Donna has been to our home, and is "family." Donna has opened her family to me as well. She has a beautiful daughter whom I have come to love, too.

Donna is such an important part of my story. When I told her that Harrison and I are writing a book, I asked her if she would just look over the rough manuscript and give me her thoughts. I knew she would. I told her that I had someone in Sacramento who is interested in co-authoring it because I knew that Donna was "retired." She had it less than a week and had the first draft back to me with her suggestions, so she and I are now on our third book. Donna and I are riding the range again for another wild ride. I could not be happier. Did I mention that I love Donna Miesbach?

As it turns out, Donna lives in Omaha, and Harrison is from Omaha, too. Because of Hummer and his impact in Nebraska, Playmakers has been doing work with kids there for about 10 years. When Harrison was still at Stanford, Donna and I already had daily afterschool programs going in the tough parts of Omaha, as well as summer camps.

Last summer, we had our first "Harrison's Playmakers" summer football camp in Omaha, and it was a huge success. We're now forming a regional board in Omaha and preparing to do year-round work. Did I mention that I am just a volunteer coach? You can do this, too. Let's do it, together. Most of you who are reading this have more than 9,000 days left.

I know I've referenced several people whom I love. I believe you can't love too many people. You may think, "Coach, you don't love people the way I love them." Here are my criteria: If I have laughed, cried, and had deep, meaningful from-the-heart conversations with someone, I may grow to love them. If we have challenged each other, have permission to speak hard truth, coached together, been fired together, been to funerals and weddings together, there is a chance I love you.

If your small Bible study group was formed over 10 years ago, and most of those guys are coaches, I may love you. A phrase that you will not hear from me is, "love ya, man." That is just another way testosterone fills men when saying "goodbye." I want to look a man in the eye, someone I have done life with, and say, "I love you." I want to look a kid in the eye and tell him or her, "I love you." I wonder what the thought bubble over your head is as I am writing about love, relationships, and coaching. If you come to Harrison's and my clinics, we will be discussing it. Does it have too much of a feminine tone to it? Are you at all feeling uncomfortable? I hope so. That's where transformation occurs.

DREAMING BIG

For the last half of 2019, the thing that has been rolling around in my mind is "playing a bigger game." As it relates to Playmakers, I have been coaching and mentoring kids for 10 years. As the Executive Director, I have been making progress, but calling it a "full time" living would be a stretch. Playing a bigger game means that we would put one of the most successful programs that we do on the shelf—our Playmakers after-school program. For the past seven years, we have had the most amazing after school program going. We have helped numerous kids in the area of academic development, behavioral development, serving in the community, and providing some tremendous opportunities for the most deserving kids. Over the years, it comes to about 1,000 kids directly.

Why would we put one of the most important programs that Playmakers does on the shelf? The answer to that, as best as I can explain it today, is because I feel like we're being called to "play a bigger game." As the Executive Director of our organization, I went to our Board and asked for permission to put our after-school program on the shelf, at least for a while. I'm fortunate to have very understanding friends serve on my Board. After numerous questions as to why, they supported that decision. The reason was because I felt our summer football camps with Harrison were taking us to a new level, and I wanted to see where God is going with that.

Our summer camps this year were extremely successful. We did four of them around the country, including Buffalo, Omaha, and two in Sacramento. Those camps reached over 400 at-risk kids and kids with special needs, and the results have been amazing. Closing the door on one thing and opening the door on another has allowed me to begin dreaming bigger.

One of those larger dreams includes a Playmakers League that addresses the deficiencies in youth sports today. The tuition to this program is a commitment of kids and families who will adhere to our Playmakers values. Those values include serving in the community. Our Playmakers kids will not play for free, but they will play because they serve in the community. Our Playmakers kids and families will be part of the Playmakers League because those kids adhere to increased academic performance and behavior.

I have this picture in my mind and heart of kids who have had difficulties in school but are improving their behavior, with teachers and administrators reporting their improvements. That energizes me! To do that, it would require Playmakers coaches who have been specially trained, somewhat compensated, and have a continuing education model that they can participate in. Specifically, this means that Playmakers coaches participate in our annual coaching clinics and receive our support materials.

I have just met with the Chief of Police in my city to begin a project where Police Officers are part of the coaching staff. This piece would offer a tremendous opportunity to our kids and families where they could begin experiencing the positive side of law enforcement. Just another step in bringing our community together.

To be part of our Playmakers League, parents would have to attend our Playmakers Parents Seminars, where we would discuss proper conduct and community service. Playmakers parents would agree to our Mission Statement that it is not about wins and losses—it's about character development. This could serve as a model that other youth organizations could begin to adopt as well. For those who cannot attend, we could do that teaching electronically.

If we continue to dream big, we will need a Playmakers facility—or Playmakers facilities—where kids with special needs can play. We are in the beginning stages of planning a second special needs facility here in Sacramento that is ADA compliant and allows these kids to play on a fair and equal playing field. The one already in place in Sacramento is the model we are following to develop a second field so more kids and families can participate. To the best of my knowledge, there is nothing like this in Buffalo today. Through Harrison's leadership, we will be looking at duplicating that in Buffalo. I can't wait to meet Buffalo Bills' Hall of Famer Jim Kelly and just dream with him about those possibilities.

For me, this is dreaming big. In addition to a special needs field for kids, Wounded Warriors and injured Veterans could utilize that facility as well. In very round numbers, it will take approximately $2,000,000 to accomplish the goal of a Playmakers League and a Playmakers field. That's a big number, but it's exciting, and I believe we can do it. The results will be unbelievable—a minimum of 500 kids and families participating in a Sports League, and that's before we add injured Veterans and Wounded Warriors.

Many of those kids will come from unemployed or under-employed families. Playmakers has partnered with adult learning facilities and vocational colleges that will partner with us. This means that the parents and relatives of our Playmakers kids will have opportunities for employment or increased vocational skills. As I think about sustainability, the results that we get from those kids in academic improvement, behavioral improvement, and class attendance will give us great quantitative and qualitative data for future funding. We have begun to tap the resources of grants in those areas, and should be able to expand those grants and financial opportunities because of the results this will generate.

For a dream as big as this to occur, first and foremost God has to be in this plan. As I mentioned earlier, my good friend, Rick Carr, said to me years ago, "Roz, you're just not smart enough to pull this off. God must be involved," and of course, he is right. I know I'm stretching my faith wings a bit and dreaming at a level that my own efforts cannot achieve. My dear friend, Harrison, will have to be part of this plan. His heart and mine have to be in sync. Even though his connections are far beyond mine, I believe that my crucial role in this plan is to continue sharing the vision. I believe that the vision is exciting enough and compelling enough that the right people are going to want to support it and be a part of our Playmakers team.

One of my favorite quotes is from the movie, "Field of Dreams," where Kevin Costner is standing in a field and hears a voice say, "If you build it, they will come." The "it" in that line is what I'm talking about—a League and facilities with coaches and parents all working together for a common cause. Surely, "if we build it, they will come!"

We're already beginning in California, Nebraska, and New York. What would it look like if we began with just a handful of coaches and kids who believe this is a worthy mission? It would be led by an uncommon man, Harrison Phillips, and an old coach who loves him and kids, and it would just grow from there. In fact, it is already beginning. Playmakers' social media platform is getting information across the nation. Other coaches from around the country are getting interested. They came to our clinics, and we bonded together. Pretty soon, other athletes like Harrison will catch the vision, too.

Corporately, we are desperate for people of character. When I talk to HR people around the country, I find it interesting that we hire people for their skills and fire them for lack of character. You can apply that same concept to your coaching staff. You need mentors of Unquestionable Character. If they have to, they can learn Inside Zone by looking at YouTube videos. Make character the non-negotiable factor. Many teams don't need more coaches, they need more character. We will show you how three men can coach forty youth kids with an organized modular practice plan. Easy!!!

If we coaches are coaching character at an early age, we'll begin cultivating better future employees. What does that look like at a youth coaching level? It means that ALL jerseys and equipment are turned in at the end of the season. That makes kids and parents more accountable early in the child's developmental process. We begin to coach the skills of being on time, playing through small hurts, and thinking "team" instead of just yourself.

~5~

SOMETHING LARGER THAN MYSELF

CHURCHES

Today I had a really awesome meeting with a coaching friend of mine who just got a new job at Mesa Verde High School. Coach Lenny and I have known each other for years and have a great relationship. Coach Lenny has the awesome job of turning around a program in a lesser-served community that has not been winning. Two years ago, his youth football program was discontinued.

Our meeting was at Starbucks, and he brought two youth football coaches with him, along with my good friend, Pastor Tim Layfield, who works with the youth at a local church. I invited Tim to coach with me two years ago to help him develop his youth program. He is a very experienced youth pastor and a wonderful coach. Today's discussion was about creating a youth football program free to kids and families in the Playmakers format. It was exciting to talk with youth coaches who are open and receptive to the idea of coaching in a different way with different objectives. We discussed how Playmakers can shape the coaching staff.

How exciting that we will begin working with these youth coaches with an entirely new model! As of right now, we're starting from scratch. We may play two games, six games, or 10 games. Today we do not know who we are going to be playing or what League we will be in. It will take somewhere in the neighborhood of $25,000 to $30,000 to pull this off. I do not know where that's going to come from, so it's going to stretch our faith to accomplish this mission.

Just think about the possibilities for a moment. A high school coach, a youth pastor, and youth football coaches meeting together at a Starbucks just discussing possibilities. Let me point out that this high school is a public high school, not a private or faith-based school. It's a school in a marginal neighborhood with little to no resources. This is where Playmakers and I want to be, and hopefully, we can make a difference. I would love to have meetings all over the country just like this one. Just imagine the possibilities. We are scheduled to meet again next week, and there will be more youth coaches at that meeting. There will also be a Saturday morning Playmakers breakfast where we will meet some of the high school players and begin putting this plan into action.

In addition to meeting two youth coaches, one of the best parts of this meeting came at the very end when a youth pastor and coach, whom I've known for five years, told me he does not attend church very often. Also, there were two youth coaches I had just met. This is an area, as a Christ follower, where I get to stretch my evangelical wings just a bit. Before we left I said to the group, "Guys, nobody is going to have a Bible under his arm on this, but you all need to know that I pray for opportunities like this on a regular basis. I personally believe we have to involve faith in what we're up to, because we can't do this on our own."

Youth coaches, these opportunities are right in front of us. I realize I'm on my soapbox here, but this kind of opportunity energizes me. I want to work with youth coaches who want to make a difference by coaching a different way. I want coaches who will objectively look at a practice plan for a 1-hour and 15-minute session so there is additional time for character development. I want to work with a high school coach who will work with a youth pastor to help him develop his youth group. Tim Layfield will do amazing things with those kids when he gets his opportunity to mentor them and pour into them. He will not pressure them. He will not hit them with the Bible. He will just be a real man, a safe place where these kids can talk and work out some of their issues. I know Harrison Phillips well enough to know that this is the kind of effort that energizes him, too. It's coaches like this and kids like this that Harrison will host a clinic and a camp for so he can encourage them to the best of his ability.

MIKE AND CHURCH

Let's talk about faith in football. There is no separation between my faith and football. Before we go further into that, I need to tell you about a man who was instrumental in changing my life, Mike Lueken. I accepted Christ into my life 22 years ago at a Promise Keepers conference in Sacramento. My brother, Jeff, who is one of the three remaining heroes in my life, played the brother card and insisted that I go, no questions asked, to a weekend conference with him. It was there that he introduced me to Franklin Graham, and I accepted an altar call and a challenge to change my life. How do you begin to thank a brother who changed the course of your life? I'm still trying to figure that out. Shortly after that event, my wife and I began going to a church called Oak Hills that was pastored by two men—Kent Carlson and Mike Lueken. Not surprisingly, both of these men play an important part in my story. Mike is one of the most intellectual, faith-based men that I know.

Mike is a football coach, trapped in a Pastor's body. Over the years, Mike has become one of my best friends and has permission to speak hard truth into my life. As our friendship has evolved, Mike takes great pleasure in doing just that. In surgical terms, he will lay me wide open and leave me there for a while just to think, and contemplate, and sort things out. I respect this man in ways that are impossible to describe.

Over these 22 years, Mike and I have shared some of my and my family's significant ups and downs. He is my life coach. Mike pastors a Church of about 1,000 people. Coincidentally, Mike is also a freshman football coach. He will say, quietly to his inner circle, that he has more influence in the community coaching freshman football than he does pastoring a church of 1,000. That has nothing to do with his ability as a pastor. He is one of the most dynamic speakers I have ever listened to. Not only do I listen to him every week, I listen to his podcasts. I read his books. I cannot get enough mentoring with him. He gives me all he can, and I am grateful.

While Playmakers is not a faith-based organization, we were birthed at my church. It has provided me, as a volunteer coach, resources far beyond mine. You may have those same resources if you make doing so a high value. As I write this, the Super Bowl is next week and my friend, Pastor Craig Sweeney from another church, has invited me to speak to his congregation on Super Bowl Sunday. I am honored and will be there. He indicated that they will be taking an "offering" at both services for Playmakers. That was not expected, but is appreciated. Pastor Craig (who coaches quarterbacks at our Playmakers Sacramento Camp) puts his church resources behind Playmakers not because of football directly, but because of how we are teaching servant leadership through football in his community.

Again, let me state that we are not a faith-based organization. We are an organization that works on public school campuses and anywhere else with any kids. It's not a coincidence that our first basketball game for kids with special needs that was berthed through Harrison was held at Oak Hills Church. If you're a coach, you need all of the resources you can get. I believe that a church—your church— can be one of those valuable resources in a God-honoring way.

You and I are just volunteer coaches with the same possibilities. You may be thinking that Playmakers is far ahead of where you may be. Maybe so, but if you commit, we can use our experience and resources to help you accelerate what you might do in your community. We would begin by having a conversation about where you are, both as a coach and geographically, and what your goals are personally and as a coach. Who knows what could happen?

My playbook (the Bible) is one example of men who have changed their destiny. I am not trying to convert the entire world to Christianity (there are far better authors who can do that). I just want to open up the potential for transforming your community through coaching and Playmakers.

If you're a volunteer coach who currently attends a church and also our clinics, let's discuss how to tap into the resources from churches and civic groups to help us mentor more kids. If you're a coach who is not yet faith-based, my strong suspicion is that you know a coach who is. I can guarantee you that a coach who knows Christ would love to take you to church and introduce you to faith in a safe and practical way. You see, I have trouble separating church and football. Or should I say faith and football. I have trouble separating faith and any category in my life. It all goes together and is part of my story.

My friend and Pastor has shaped my life. He has coached me and pastored me in my transformation through faith. He has shown me what a transparent man and a transparent coach looks like. If my Pastor can stand in front of a congregation and speak openly about his flaws as a man, husband, and Christ follower, then I can do the same. I can also use that as a coaching moment by standing in front of my team and being transparent. I can tell my team that I made a mistake. My Pastor makes mistakes (he's a Packers fan). He is still being transformed, and he models that for me in the most real and honest manner I have ever seen.

Have you ever known a coach who could not say he was wrong? Who made a mistake and could not say he was sorry? I have. Mike models transparency for me. He shows me what it looks like. So stand in front of your team (your congregation), and be real. Be human and say you are sorry. That is a man I can follow. That is just a glimpse of Mike Lueken, my friend, and a man I love. I think he loves me, too. We're just two volunteer coaches woven together through faith and football.

Coaches, this is not just a series of coincidences. Meeting the Harrisons, Donna, Mike Lueken, the Bills, and more are not just cosmic events. You can't believe that. This is faith, a great game, and you as a volunteer coach, having an opportunity of a lifetime.

Today, we live in a "post-Christian" society. This means that most people in our society have had the opportunity to know about faith and Christ. It is not a new story, yet Christianity is being pushed into the margin of our lives more than ever. People are leaving the church at an alarming rate. God has been eliminated from school, and we don't say the Pledge of Allegiance any longer. I just asked over 100 coaches, "Why are fewer kids playing sports today?" And my question to you is this: "How's all that working for us?" I suggest that overall it is not working very well.

What is a solution? How about beginning with a handful of coaches who believe that their team is a "congregation"? Your team is a small church, and YOU are the pastor. Over time, this idea could expand so it includes more coaches all over the country. My friend and high school coach, Lenny, has just taken over a team and a youth football program at a small high school. He already leads a small congregation that will have about 200 kids and families involved. That is the average size of a church in America today. He has a following. We are now meeting with him, his staff, and youth coaches to make sure we are leading those kids and families with Playmakers core values: Academics, Family, Serving Others, and Winning with Honor. What would it look like if 10 Lenny's showed up at Harrison's and my clinics this year? How about 100? Maybe more, who knows? I am crazy enough to believe that it is coaches—volunteer coaches—who are going to change the trajectory of kids and families for a lifetime. I get an opportunity to do it alongside Bigfoot because we have faith and relationship, through football.

A MODERN-DAY PROPHET

I believe Joe Ehrmann is a modern-day profit. He teaches, and I concur, that we have been given the wrong information. What do you think of when you hear the word, "masculinity"? How would you define it? I, like many young men, learned it the wrong way. Masculinity was first introduced to me on the ball field. Because I was bigger and the first one picked on the elementary school field, I was told that I was a "stud." Because I was the captain, I got the attention, so I was "the man." The last guys picked were the sissies and afraid to hit. False masculinity was being formed, and I did not know it.

Now move to puberty and then to high school. Let's just say that I was an "early adaptor" in this area. I was talked about in the locker room, and my "false masculinity" was further formed. I did not have a model at home who was modeling and communicating with me about how a real man treats and respects a woman. It was not coached and modeled, so I "figured it out" all by myself through a trial and error method. It was more testosterone-based learning. I was the high school quarterback, gifted with my mom's looks and wanting to score on and off the field. Others like me were doing the same. If you were not good with all that as a 16-year-old, you were put into a feminine category. You were non-masculine. That's 10,000 miles from being right, but that is the way it was, and still is today.

In many instances we men are off the rails. Look at the support agencies that exist due to the pain we have caused:

- W.E.A.V.E. (Women Escaping A Violent Environment)
- Foster Parents
- Child Protective Services
- Single Mom's Strong

This is just a handful of the agencies that are here to help undo what we men have done to others. This isn't very pleasant, and you may not think it is relevant in a coaches' book. I would present that it is MANDATORY that we look into these areas and make a stand.

Joe Ehrmann's story in "Season of Life" and his further teachings have taught me a definition of masculinity that is a "true north" for me. He defines masculinity as "A DEEP AND MEANINGFUL RELATIONSHIP WITH ANOTHER MAN, AND BEING A CHAMPION FOR SOMETHING LARGER THAN YOURSELF." Apparently, not many people know this. I say that because there are shelves of books, both faith-based and secular, written on the loneliness of the men in our society. Joe's definition could solve that.

As I have mentioned, I am 63 years old, and have been married to my best friend, Miss Linda, for 26 years. Through the grace of God, I am a cancer survivor and a volunteer coach. Three years ago, I wrote (and am still rewriting) my 30-year life plan. Yes, I can do math. That will take me up to about 90-ish. I know that when my time comes, it comes. Until it does, there are kids to coach and mentor, there are new relationships to cultivate, and there is also one to mature. The common thread, for me, is my faith, football, and relationships, including those already existing and those to come. I have a Players Tree to grow and watch that tree bear fruit. There are more weddings, more kids, more funerals, and baptisms. Unless He takes me home early, I have about 9,000 days left, and I don't want to be asking for overtime. I want to squeeze every drop out of this volunteer coaching that I can.

THE MOST CHALLENGING CHAPTER

I hope that by reading this you will want to become a Playmakers coach. I hope you will challenge yourself to go the distance. I hope you'll commit to 12 months (one season) of doing things differently. You may be amazed at what happens, and how those 12 months will reshape not only your coaching philosophy but also how you do the rest of your life.

I want to meet regionally and nationally with you coaches so we can encourage one another and brainstorm what is working across the nation. We can form bonds that include laughing and crying together. We can support our relational wins and learn from our losses. Coaches of great character and winners on the field, come and coach us up. Let's do it at a place where we can have fun. Is anyone reading this having too much fun right now? Let's try this together for 12 months, and see what happens. We will invite Bigfoot, and he will be there cheering us on and helping us all he can.

As I have said, I have the lofty goal of helping coaches all over the country reshape their coaching model and assisting them through Playmakers in getting some funding for themselves to offset their personal expenses. I want you to have at least some money for gas and some Saturday pizzas so you can spend extra time with the kids you'll be mentoring. I believe our plan will help you do that. We can do this together, both legally and ethically, so you can expand your influence in your community. This plan will help you in your continuing education by attending our seminars and staying abreast of the most effective mentoring and coaching techniques.

I'm asking you to pray to our God to give you the direction and the courage to coach through faith. My prayer is that you will be courageous and make no secret that you are using faith in mentoring these kids and the players on your team. I realize how risky that is. I believe we need to take this risk. As I am writing this here in my living room, I am watching the national news tell about a father attacking his son's opponent at a high school wrestling match. In my heart, I believe we need bold people, and we need people who are willing to take a risk now more than ever. We need more Harrison Phillips. Here are the action steps I'm suggesting.

Take some time and get into a quiet place and write your personal mission statement. It doesn't have to be perfect. It just needs to be a first draft. Get inspired and be bold. I have included Merlin Olsen's mission statement below. Read it. Yours doesn't have to match Merlin Olsen's, but that would be a tremendous start and it could inspire you:

> *The focus of my life begins with family, loved ones, and friends. I want to use my resources to create a secure environment that fosters love, learning, laughter, and mutual success. I will protect and value integrity. I will admit and quickly correct my mistakes. I will be a self-starter. I will be a caring person. I will be a good listener with an open mind. I will continue to grow and learn. I will facilitate and celebrate the success of others.*
>
> *(Merlin Olsen)*

Have the courage to declare that you are going to be a Playmakers coach. Begin with your wife or someone close to you. Then go to your local coaching network and tell them that you aspire to be a Playmakers coach. I can assure you they're going to be curious about what that is.

Your next step is to get on Playmakers' and Harrison's social media and begin communicating your intentions to become a Playmakers coach. Find out where our coaching seminars are going to be held and begin planning to attend. Our social media information is included in this book. I promise you this is exactly how I began. I read a book about Joe Ehrmann which inspired me to be a lifelong mentor and coach. Not only did he inspire me, he offered specific tools that helped me begin a new process in coaching. I told anyone who would listen, how I was going to mentor and coach. Very soon, two other coaches, who were good friends of mine, became very curious and wanted to do the same, and so the process began.

I believe that every person's life is worthy of journaling. I'm going to encourage you to buy a journal and begin making notes about what's happening as you begin this process. Journaling is not easy, but coaching is not easy either. Let me say again that your life is worth writing about. It is a story, and it needs to be documented. Each one of our kids has a story and their stories need to be documented, too. There needs to be a trail—a written trail—about how we changed the trajectory of youth all over the country.

At our meeting, I will hand you a journal so you can begin writing about an amazing person's life that is worthy of documenting. His name is Coach (fill your name in here). Yes, I'm talking about you. People will want to know your story. And while you're at it, you can also write about the people who have influenced you.

I want you to think about what your personal network looks like. When you begin the process of securing funding for your coaching, you will need to expand your personal network. Here are some suggestions about how to do that. First, begin with your personal network. That means writing down at least 30 names of people you can have a one on one conversation with. After you have contacted us, we will send you Playmakers' information which you can share with them. It will tell how you're going to mentor and coach kids this year. It will lay out the expenses involved, the things you will be doing to assist the kids, and the modest amount of money it will take to do that. You're going to invite them to partner with you. This is how I began 10 years ago, with a core group of one-time funders or monthly funders who believed in what I was up to. Please don't shy away from this. People want to be involved in an inspiring cause, and you are going to be an inspiring cause. In addition to your personal network, if you attend church, visit with your pastor, and let him know what you're up to. You want your church's involvement as well.

How familiar are you with civic groups like Rotary, Optimists, and Kiwanis? These are tremendous civic organizations that are based in your city. If you're not familiar with them, they are a group of businesspeople, both active and retired, with the mission of helping people in the community in a variety of different ways. I have spoken to almost 100 civic groups throughout the country about Playmakers. Many of them support my organization. Civic organizations support me corporately, and people from my church support me both corporately and individually. Over time they will do the same for you. When you contact Playmakers, we will send you all of the necessary information and support materials to get you going with this endeavor.

Coach, we're going to develop a relationship together through Playmakers. In God's time, we will meet. You will begin influencing coaches in your network. That may be your team. It may be the organization that you coach for. Eventually it could become an entire League. At the right place and the right time, invite me to come and speak to your organization. Playmakers does Youth Coaching Certifications all over the country, and we welcome opportunities to come and meet you. We can establish a goal of setting a Playmakers location within your city. We've done that in Sacramento California, Omaha Nebraska, and Buffalo New York. You may become our next Playmakers hub. I get excited just thinking about the possibilities.

Let me say one more time that I began as a volunteer coach, just like you. God has gifted me with a desire to create relationships, to get to know more people, and to try to mentor young people. My guess is He has gifted you in the same way. I am 63 years old, a cancer survivor, a follower of Christ, and a former football player. All of those pieces have converged into how I choose to spend the rest of my life, and I invite you to explore those same opportunities.

The stakes are too high for us not to go the distance on this. Today in our country, two out of five kids are living in a home without their biological father. One-third of the kids in our country are living with a single mom or a single parent. One hundred thousand kids in our country today are carrying guns to school. Almost half the kids in our country do not read at grade level in third grade. We have an epidemic of a fatherless society. Give me some indications where things are improving? More kids today are playing video games and fewer kids are participating in sports. When was the last time you saw two kids playing catch on a front lawn?

Who are we going to look to, to create the next generation of leaders? Where is the next Walter Payton going to come from? Who is going to remind our kids about the heroes of 9-11? Who is going to tell them about the firefighters who refused to stop digging on 9-11 after they were told that there was no longer any hope for survivors? Who will tell our young kids who grow up to be leaders that four planes went down on 9-11? Or that one of the passengers by the name of Todd Beamer showed immediate leadership by forming a small team at the back of the plane? That he inspired that small group of men to help him take over the cockpit? That he said the Lord's Prayer, and together they charged the cockpit, possibly keeping that plane from flying into the White House?

We need more Harrison Phillips. We need men who go to the Children's Hospital, not just for show, but to speak and meet with kids who are forgotten. We need men like Harrison to show other professional athletes how it's done, and our job is to share the story. I believe this is why we're called to coach, why we are called to mentor, and why we must create quality relationships. We must show kids how to show their heart and their emotions in healthy ways, and teach them how to be real men—men who are kind, gentle, loving, and compassionate.

This is just a handful of the inspirational stories that our leaders need to understand. We can't depend on schools to teach it because things become too controversial. We can't say a prayer in school anymore. We can't say the Pledge of Allegiance. We need leaders. We need coaches. We need inspirational men who can be trusted to get things back on the rails. We need you.

I hope I get to meet Bill McCartney, founder of Promise Keepers and former head coach at the University of Colorado. I want to ask him if he had a business plan laid out and organized in such a manner that he knew it would be a movement that would spread across the country using football stadiums as God's platform. I want to know if he had all of that thought out, or if he was just one coach with the courage to do things differently.

I want to meet Dabo Swinney. I want to meet his players. I want to ask them if Coach really loves them the way he says he does on TV. I want to believe that he does. I want to believe that Coach Swinney truly cares about his players at a level that is uncommon.

I want you to meet and coach beside my friend, Coach Warren Keller. Coach Keller coaches the Fremont School for the Deaf. He is completely deaf, and he coaches a team that is deaf. He is one of the most inspirational men I have ever met. We have coached at Playmakers camps together for the past seven years, and he teaches me so much. I want you to experience watching and participating beside a deaf coach. I want you to see how he communicates with his team, and how he shows love to them. It will inspire you.

We can also learn together from my good friend, Coach Rick Garretson. Coach Garretson and I are Aztecs and have known each other for over 30 years. Rick is a lifetime coach and is the head coach at Chandler High School, which also happens to be the Arizona State Champs. Coach Garretson does it the right way, with class, integrity, and high standards.

Or you may have an opportunity to meet Coach Jody Sears. Coach Sears is the former head coach at Sacramento State and instills character and love in his program at a Division One level. I had the opportunity to see this up close and personal. Coach Sears has given me hours of his time. He has spoken at many of our Playmakers dinners and has inspired both coaches and players to do great things. I am privileged to call Coach Sears a friend.

These are just some of the relationships I have developed and cherished over my lifetime. They are the richness in my life, and each day gets better because of them. It is fun for me to write about my relationships and coaching experiences, but I want to know about yours—both in the past and the ones to come. The question is, I want to know what are you going to do moving forward? We both have read books that we finish and think, "That's nice, I got some good suggestions," and you move on. Rarely have those books had a lifelong impact on me. I am not suggesting that what I am writing is the coaching "Holy Grail." Remember, I am just a volunteer coach, just like you. (Have I mentioned that?)

I will also admit that there are times when I read the Bible that it just seems like words on a page. I wish I could tell you that reading the Bible is easy and that I devour it each and every day. That is just not the case for me, but there are times when I pick it up and re-read something I have read many times before, and it speaks to my heart. My prayer is that will happen for you, too.

In the book of Acts (my favorite book of the Bible), there is a character named Saul who was paid by the Romans to extinguish Christianity. He was a bad dude. Through an encounter with The Living God, he was assigned a mentor (a coach), and over time he was transformed into a "new man" called Paul. Paul (the author of one-fourth of the New Testament) changed the world when he was transformed into a new man.

Coaches, we can be transformed into new men, too. We can be new coaches and change the world. As Todd Beemer said just before storming the cockpit on 9-11, LETS ROLL!!

PHOTO ALBUM

Roz with Coach Garret Wolfe, Director of Football Operations at Sacramento State University

Roz and Linda with Harrison and Jordan

Harrison at Stanford

Roz, with Harrison's mom, Tammie

PHOTO ALBUM | 75

Roz & Harrison at the Bills' stadium receiving the
My Cause-My Cleats Award

*With Mrs. Ralph Wilson, former Bills owner
and wonderful community supporter*

*Roz and Blake. Blake serves on the
Playmakers' Kids Board in Buffalo*

*Chief Petty Officer Jason Martz, one of our original
Playmakers kids, now husband and father*

At the Omaha Camp

Playmakers serving in the Sacramento community

"She chose me. God is big."

"The other woman in my life" – Donna

PHOTO ALBUM | 79

Roz with Warren Keller, Head Coach at the California School for the Deaf

Linda and I with life-long friend, Coach Rick Garretson and his wife, Wendy and son, Darrell

*Roz and Donna with David Humm
and Hummer's daughter, Courtney*

Standing on top of the world (at Children's Hospital, Buffalo)

Harrison with the Bills

*Harrison and Jordan –
Stanford Grads and Playmakers Forever*

"Why Playmakers – A Nonprofit with God at the Center"

Kids camp at the Bills stadium

Autographing at a Buffalo hospital

"Why I am Passionate about Paying It Forward"

84 | BEYOND COACHING

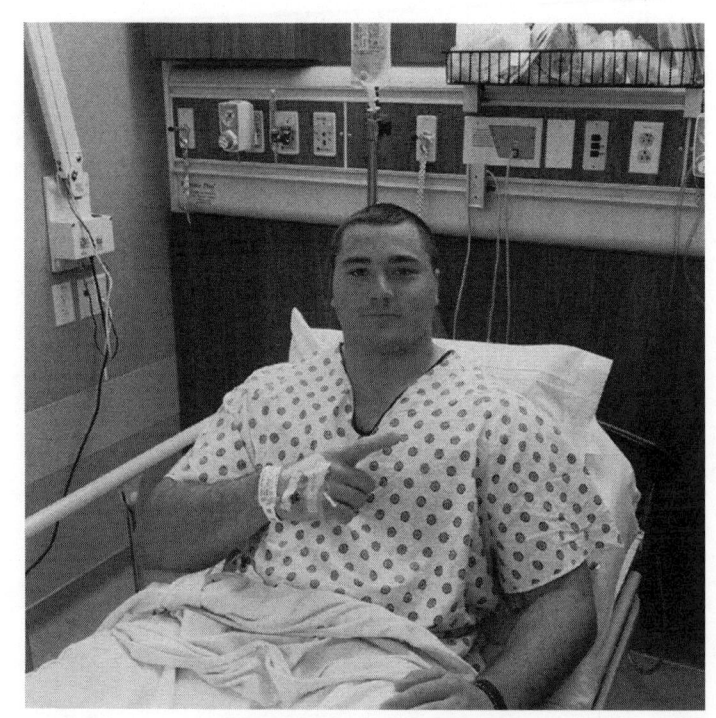

In for knee surgery

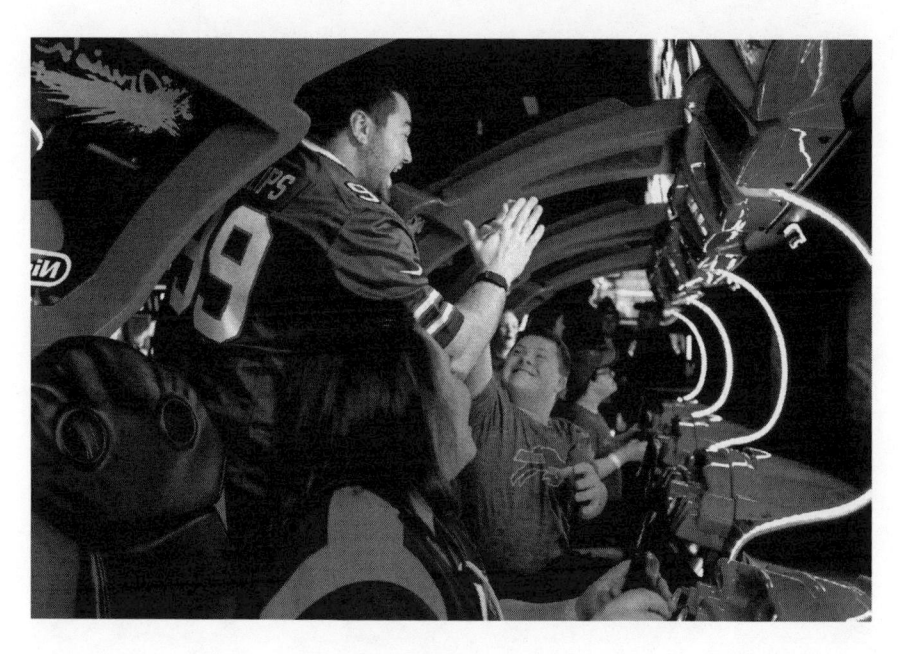

Special Needs Kids

At the Omaha Camp

Omaha Camp (Photo courtesy of JessieMarie)

Omaha Camp

More Camp pictures

Tug of War

Wheelchair Dancing

PART TWO

TACKLING LIFE

BY HARRISON PHILLIPS,
BUFFALO BILLS
DEFENSIVE TACKLE

INTRODUCTION

Before I get started, there are two things I must note. First, I am truly curious to see how a book written by two men at the same time without communication will turn out, especially since we're 40 years apart in age. Yes, he's 63 and I'm 23. I said I'd be interested in writing a book about the amazing things we are learning through the children we work with. He thought it was a good idea, so he said something along the lines of, "Write about our relationship, your story, our kids, and the way we coach, and I'll do the same." That's all the information I got, and away I go...

Second, I want you to know this book is almost a rough draft for me. As I write here and there, with small ideas popping into my head, I believe this is just a start. I'll use some of this short book, co-authored with my Playmakers team, as a blueprint to expand into a much vaster book of my own, hopefully after I lift up a Lombardi trophy. So if you ever re-read some of this book down the road, don't give me too hard of a time. I'm a busy guy, so I may copy and paste a little.

~1~

RELATIONSHIP WITH ROZ AND JORDAN

When I think about the relationships I have with people, I think of times spent together. By that, I mean together in the same room. Laughs, cries, joy, whatever the case may be, when I think of the people I feel closest to, I think of the moments we've shared together. It's easy to see why I am close with my family—I lived with them for 18 years. My best friends, I've known for 12-plus years, spending thousands of hours together. Teammates I work with 10 hours a day. I find many memories and experiences when I think of these relationships. That's why my relationship with Greg is different.

Greg and I don't go way back. Greg and I don't have countless logged memories. We've been working together since 2014, so the memories are starting to build, but for the relationship to start so rapidly, it didn't make sense. It goes to show how opening your heart—and generosity—can expedite many things in life. For me, it expedited a new friendship.

When I showed up at Stanford campus bright-eyed and bushy-tailed, I didn't fully understand what I was getting into. I am DRIVEN. I find value and worth in work ethic. Therefore, I am chronically competitive, constantly trying to work harder, put in more time, and find new things to master. Stanford was the best, and the worst, place for this drive.

Stanford provided more opportunities than I could ever have imagined. That helped me climb to heights I'd never dreamed of, but it cost me a lot. Happiness, joy, relaxation, boredom, and social life suffered in many ways due to this drive. When signing up for classes, I heard a teammate say he'd be taking 16 credits for his first quarter of college. (Fifteen credit hours is a normal student course load to graduate in four years). Sixteen credits might not seem like much, but that's during the Fall quarter, our football season. It's hard to calculate how many hours I spend at football each week without getting the NCAA in any trouble. Technically it's only 20 hours. When you add all the recovery, extra film, rehab and training room work, lifts that run long, extra work on the practice field, eating, getting to and from the facility, and traveling for games, we're talking almost 60 hours a week I'm in football activities. Due to this fact, many students take a summer school class to lighten the fall quarter. Most football players only take about 12 credit hours in season.

Hearing another teammate was taking 16, the drive in me made me sign up for 17. Then, when I was in my freshman dorm and heard a student jabbing about the 19 credits he signed up for, I decided to pick up one more class and cap it off at 20, which is the maximum amount allowed to be taken in a quarter. Why not? Hard work can accomplish anything. While I was always grinding academically, I knew football was my dream and my future. It was what kept me up at night and kept me humbled.

There was a player who was just named captain of our team—Senior safety Jordan Richards. This guy seemed to have it. You know when you see someone and they just have all their stuff together. They just have positive energy radiating off them. That was my dog, J Rich. If Stanford had a Clark Kent, it would be Jordan. He was smart, caring, a man of Christ, and an incredibly talented football player. I knew from the moment I stepped on campus and saw the way he handled his business, this was the guy to follow.

I learned a valuable thing when I got drafted to the Bills. A coach they called Bullet said to me, "As a rookie, it's better to be seen than heard, because if you're heard, you're not seen." In other words, shut up and watch how it's done. Rookies have to prove themselves before they get the right to talk. Without knowing it, I tried to do that my freshman year at Stanford. I would always follow around the older guys and emulate what they did. Jordan was a very hard worker, so we were usually the last ones off the field, or the last ones in the weight room. That sparked many great conversations and good memories.

I think it was the first week I got to Stanford that Jordan told me about the Christian Life group on campus. We did a football Bible study that he and I ran. We also worked very closely in forming the fellowship of Christian Athletes with some other athletes on campus. They had no athlete group prior to that. That group still meets to this day. You may always be able to go back and find our names in the stat books, but one of our biggest accomplishments is that we helped create a group that still meets seven years later with 50-plus student-athletes.

One day Jordan and I were talking about our faith upbringing. He mentioned to me a fellow named Coach Roz, that he was a good man who was always there with a helping hand. Nothing much else came up about Coach Roz until Jordan pulled me aside after a game one night. We have a family area at the top of our tunnel on home games. We just won, and we were feeling pretty good. I was trying to search for my folks when Jordan said he wanted to introduce me to his family friend, Coach Roz.

I quickly went over and said hello to Terry and Sharon Richards as well as Coach Roz and his wife, Miss Linda. They seemed like very kind and caring people, people you'd go out of your way to help move, if they ever asked. After a short conversation, Greg was pleased to hear I was a man of faith. He told me, from what he's seen, I am an uncommon man and encouraged me to keep living life that way. Then out of the blue, he said if I ever need to get away and want to breathe for a weekend, and have a home-cooked meal, I'm welcome at their home anytime. I thought, what a polite thing to say, but when he gave me his number and said it again in a dead-serious tone, I knew he wasn't bluffing. I laughed it off and said, "Nice to meet you," and hugged them both goodbye before going to find my family. I thought it was strange for him to offer that off of a three-minute conversation, but hey, this is California. Things are just different here.

The next day, I caught up with JR and asked about the Roeszlers. He told me more about Greg and Linda. It was great to hear about the cool things Greg was doing up in the Sac area with youth. Jordan highly recommended that I actually go up there and stay with them.

This was still bizarre to me, but I saved his number. After the season, Jordan left to train for the NFL. We were in winter conditioning, working out for hours every day, and I had six new classes and 20 credits to work with. After a month of the same routine of grind, grind, grind, Greg reached out and reminded me of the offer, so I decided to see what this was all about. I told Greg I'd make the trip as long as I got the chance to meet some of the kids he coaches and works with. Two days later, after an exhausting focus and finish Friday work out (focus and finish pretty much translates to hard as hell), I packed a bag and Ubered to a train stop. I boarded a train for the first time in my life, got out my laptop and typed a paper on my four-hour ride to Sacramento. When I arrived, I walked a long walk out of the train station, and called Greg to ask if he was there.

I'm not sure why, but I had this impression that this couple was wealthy. Like really wealthy. I remember telling my girlfriend I was going to stay at some mansion in Sac. Maybe I thought they were rich because it seems like everyone at Stanford games are rich. Maybe because Greg worked with kids, I assumed he was Financially Stable enough to not work. Maybe it was because they said I could stay in their home, making me think they had a plethora of space and bedrooms for me. Maybe because they were older and dressed nice when I met them. All I know is, that wasn't the case.

When I called Greg, asking if he was there, he (of course) was running late. I've learned since then that Greg running late is not abnormal. Even after the texts at each train stop on the way, letting him know exactly when I'd be there, I still had to wait a good 20 minutes until he arrived. I got the call he had just pulled up, but I was outside and didn't see any nice cars pulling up. Then I heard a honk and saw Greg waving out of his 2006 Lexus SUV that had 250,000 miles on it. This was not the BMW or Mercedes I was picturing.

The conversation was light and easy on the ride home. It was dark out, so I didn't quite see where we were going. Greg stopped at the "In-N-Out" on the way home and got me two double-doubles. Now I knew for sure Greg was a good dude.

When we pulled into the neighborhood, I knew my expectations of a multi-million dollar home was wrong. We parked in the driveway and got out of the car. The house was a nice, small, single-family home. I wasn't unappreciative, I just wasn't expecting it. We walked into the house and was pointed to the couch where I'd be sleeping for the next two nights. It wasn't a big deal to me. I was smaller back then, almost 60 pounds smaller.

I was so shocked at how generous he was with everything, inviting a complete stranger into his home where his daughter and wife were sleeping. We talked for a few minutes, then he went to bed. I FaceTimed my girlfriend, and we had a good laugh at the situation I got myself into. How did I end up on a couch in the outskirts of Sacramento, in the home of someone I'd only met for three minutes? I guess I just took a leap of faith.

Call it what you want, but Greg and I sparked a cool friendship that weekend. I got spoiled by Miss Linda, and made the day for a bunch of kids by stopping in and hanging out with them for a bit. Some were even Stanford fans. When we woke up for church Sunday, I knew these guys were the real deal. They were welcomed by everyone at church, and seemed to have a great community there. It was inspiring. I hoped that I, too, in 30 years or so, would have a church community like that.

After that weekend, I felt I had a good base to start building a connection with them, but it happened much faster than you'd think. After a three-minute conversation, I spent a weekend with them, and after three days, we were already working together. I'm pretty sure he texted me he loved me after that. Not in a creepy way, but in the protective, brother-in-Christ way. It was cool to have a family away from family. It's just crazy how it all started so randomly.

Now, we're six years later, and are touching the lives of thousands. Harrison's Playmakers are all over the United States: West Coast, check! East Coast, check! Midwest, check! Greg and I have seen each other in person maybe 30 days in our entire lives, but through opening your heart, generosity, and drive, a lot of good has come from it.

Greg and I dream in the same atmosphere. We're just on different planets. I am a huge advocate for dreaming big far off dreams, and doing whatever you can to accomplish them. Greg is that on steroids. I like to take baby steps, then move into walking, then jogging, then a sprint. Greg would start a marathon with a full sprint.

Regardless, one of my favorite quotes states, "If you reach for the stars, and only get to the clouds, you're still higher than everyone else." That is where we are trying to take Playmakers today. The dream is to work with thousands and thousands of children with developmental differences and special needs, bringing them nothing but joy, new experiences, inclusion, friendship, and teaching them to pay it forward. We are gearing up and planning our 2020 camp tour, hoping to get 1,000 kids at our three Playmakers football camps (Buffalo, Omaha, Sacramento), as well as planning year-round activities, such as Bills games, dinners, scholarships, etc. Greg thinks that next year we can be in 50 states with 10,000 kids working with us in each state. (That may be a little exaggeration.) All joking aside, he dreams big, and only good can come from it. I encourage everyone to dream this big.

~2~

WHY PLAYMAKERS— A NONPROFIT WITH GOD AT THE CENTER

For any successful college football player, and especially an NFL player, you will be contacted by hundreds of non-profits. It's not a bad thing at all, it can just be stressful at times. It's great to see so many people caring about different causes, but it sucks knowing you can't help all of them. I've worked with many organizations, and I still do to this day, but Playmakers is the one I've decided to make my own and call home.

No doubt you are familiar with the Playmakers by now, but I feel like I should explain why I chose this one. There are three big reasons:

1. Working on literacy skills with at-risk youth
2. Character development
3. Physical activity

These are all things I am passionate about. Obviously, as an athlete, I enjoy working out, but it's more than that. I understand how important being physically fit is. The overall lifetime health benefits are too extreme not to care. We're in a world eating itself to death, so encouraging these kids to exercise is huge. Not only does this burn calories, this also gives kids new opportunities to play new sports and activities. Through Playmakers, many kids have played soccer for the first time, and years later are now playing in high school. Sports are so beneficial to kids. I am happy we have that component.

Improving literacy skills is also extremely important to me. One of my majors at Stanford was sociology, and my minor was in education. I learned so much about the achievement gap and the issues in most inner-city schools. With almost 50% of kids reading below grade level, something has to be done. I think that coaching youth about reading, and making their learning experience enjoyable and fun, will help us close this gap.

I saw first-hand how the Playmakers literacy program works. The kids love it. Coaches are having to almost pull kids back because of how fast they want to go. It's beautiful.

Lastly, the character development. We need a video to go with this book for you to fully understand how powerful the character development component is. The change I've seen in Playmakers pups in just a handful of years is incredible. To see a kid who won't look you in the eye, causing big distractions in class, and never doing any work, transform into a mature, well rounded young man is jaw-dropping. It restores faith in humanity.

The special thing about the character development piece is that these values and lessons are similar to those in the Bible, so we're in public schools teaching very similar topics and morals as the Bible does. This was my first time seeing a nonprofit take advantage of this gray area to show these kids the Christ-like way of life.

~3~

SHORTCOMINGS

As I write about some of the accomplishments in my life, I don't want this to seem egotistical. I have no desire for this to be the case. I've prayed about how this book will make me seem to the public, and in all reality, it doesn't matter. God knows my heart; he knows there is little to no arrogance in these words. In the long run, this is a book to help kids, and if I have to come across as cocky for you to understand my situation, so be it. Just know it's not a brag, it's just how God has blessed me.

By the time I hit high school I was a fairly well developed young man. I was about 6'3" and 190 pounds. Big for a 14-year-old. For every part of me that looked mature there was an equal part who could act it. My parents did an amazing job at teaching me social skills and how to be a gentleman. My folks are the reason I am where I am today. One thing I appreciate most is their forcing me to attend Sunday school every week.

My relationship with church was a roller coaster. There were times as a kid when I loved it, and just wanted to go make a big fish with some arts and crafts when we were told the story of Jonah. Then I'd have a period where I just wanted to skip it so I could go to a wrestling practice, or hang out with friends. My parents were good at keeping me engaged in my faith. We prayed together at night before every meal, and when I was young, they prayed with me in bed at night.

My church was Lutheran, so confirmation can start in sixth grade. They have a regimen to follow, which allows you to finish at a normal pace in three years, I believe. You start at the beginning of sixth, and finish at the end of eighth, taking a class once a week on a Wednesday or Saturday night. Well, at this time in my life, I was on fire for the Lord. I loved learning the history, and also about my Lord and Savior. I flew through the gospels in the first week of class. Long story short, I completed confirmation in the first year. I was the only kid my age who finished that fast. It was fun, because now I could just go to church with my family on Sundays, no more extra classes and meetings.

Unfortunately, over the few next years, I lost the spark that fueled my diving deep into my faith. I've never lost faith or doubted Jesus as my Savior. I just didn't do anything to learn more. After confirmation, I thought I had it made, so I'd pray before I ate, at bedtime, and before any athletic competition, but during the next couple of years, I sinned a lot. I'm a big sinner. We all are, except One. However, for some reason, those young adult years were my bad boy, big man on campus, fake male bravado days.

As middle school ended, I was one of the most highly recruited 14-year-olds. Not to colleges, but to high schools. Yes! Even in little ol' Omaha, Nebraska, we still have high schools recruiting middle school kids to go out of the district to their school. I had five high schools contact me about going to their school. They would pick me up and drop me off every day if they had to. I knew from the get-go that I wanted to stay at my neighborhood school with my neighborhood friends. It's the right thing to do, plus my sister was going to be a senior.

Right off the bat I was driven to be the best athlete whoever walked through the doors. And I had confidence. Those days, I was truly cocky. I hadn't been humbled yet. I would tell anyone who asked, "I'm going to be a state champion wrestler, go D1 for football, and play in the NFL." Kids would laugh at that or talk behind my back about how cocky I was. I was just a firm believer that I could work hard enough for it to happen. At the time, I can see how it rubbed people the wrong way. I wish it hadn't, because I lost a handful of friends because of it. That's also the reason I'm in the NFL today.

My freshman year was mainly a year of great potential. I had a great football season, but an even better wrestling season. When I made varsity, I started hanging around the other guys in varsity. This was mainly the seniors. Everyone knows high school involves some drinking and drugs. I wish it wasn't the case, but that's the world we live in. Those 18-year-old seniors made me grow up fast. At 14, I was partaking in the same partying they were. It was fun, new, and I wanted to be cool.

What a terrible little world we live in during high school where you brag about how blacked out drunk you got, how high you were, drunk driving, all of it. I was a part of it, too. It's not a good thing. I'm not proud of it, but those are some of the best, most vivid memories I have, and with my best friends, none the less. To this day, I'll catch myself thanking God that nothing terrible happened to us kids. It's a miracle. We had a designated drunk driver. Yes, you read that right. We had a buddy who we decided was the best drunk driver, so he would drive if we were all drinking. It was innocent. In that small world you live in, you have zero idea of consequences. You feel invincible.

My friend group wasn't a typical party group from a movie. We didn't drink on weeknights or have serious drugs on us. We were actually known by most parents, teachers, and adults, as the good kids. We were all Eddie Haskells. We knew how to shoot the bull, and talk our way out of anything. These guys were all smart, went on to get full-ride scholarships, and currently have good-paying jobs. That's probably why we never got caught with anything over those years. That combination of being smart, an athlete, and a good talker are probably why we had a lot of success with women as well.

I had a girlfriend for over a year in my sophomore year of high school. It was a typical first relationship. Most of my friends had a girlfriend, so I wanted one, too. She was sweet, and it was a good first relationship. When that relationship ended, I was known pretty well around the area. I had won a state championship in wrestling, and was an All-State football player with multiple division one scholarships.

Division one is rare in Nebraska. You'd normally get one or two kids a year that could go D1. Most of them would go to Nebraska. When the summer came, I had over 20 scholarships to different schools for football, and was a national champion wrestler—and I was single.

I treated a lot of really nice, beautiful girls poorly. I was caught up in living a "superstar" life as a successful athlete in high school. I had forgotten what being a gentleman was, and had completely forgotten how a Christ-like man should act. It sickens me to think about the time I was proud of this, but my parents used to call our front door "the revolving door" because girl after girl would just come in and come out. My parents thought these were friends or classmates. Maybe they knew I was fooling around a bit, but they would never have expected everything that happened. Otherwise, they wouldn't have allowed it.

I was trapped in the male locker room my whole life where all we heard about was the new girl a guy had sex with. It starts as early as middle school. I'd go up to the high school to work out at 11 years old and hear the seniors talking about how many girls they've gotten with, and making fun of the guys who hadn't gotten with many. It's instilled in you that being cool and having sex go hand in hand. I'm not making excuses for my behavior. I'm just saying I was a product of my environment.

To this day I feel terrible for the things I did back then. These good girls didn't deserve to be treated the way I treated them. In no way will I ever be proud to tell my daughter these stories one day. It sickens me that I'll have to protect her from people like the kid I was.

These are my biggest shortcomings in life. If I could relive those years, I'd do it in a second. I'd change a lot. Unfortunately, I cannot do that. I've prayed for forgiveness many times. I wish it could erase some pain I caused others.

What saved me from continuing to be such a jerk was actually—another girl. I called her Superstar. This was a girl I'd had my eye on for a very long time. She was a runner, so I would see her running outside almost every day when I was working out. She was known by my friends as a girl too hard to get. She wasn't like the normal field we ran around with. She was quiet, innocent, and younger. I always said hi to her and tried to present my best self whenever she was around. I guess I was laying some groundwork for years before we actually started to date.

During my time with the revolving door, she was a girl that I'd invite over. Her visits were very different than some of the other girls. She would sit on a couch separate from mine, no cuddling, no being under the same blanket. The lights were always on, and she would rarely talk. I had to initiate any and all conversation. It was my job to make her comfortable, and crack some of her shyness. It was a lot of work. I think that's what I liked the most. The challenge of trying to get her. It was different. She wasn't a girl you kissed on the first date, mainly because you couldn't even get close enough. My friends would call that being a prude; I would just call it innocent and mature at the same time. She clearly didn't grow up similarly, or as fast, as I did.

✲✲✲

After a few weeks, I must have felt defeated that things weren't moving faster. Football season was starting up, and I still had a handful of girls I was interested in. I came to find out later that the reason things were moving so slowly with her was because she suspected me of fooling around with other girls. Anyway, she and I drifted apart. The revolving door stayed revolving for most of the football season and into the winter. I still thought about Superstar often. Since prom was approaching, I knew I'd have to settle down and go with one girl.

For homecoming, my best friend and I went as each other's dates. The reason none of our teammates or classmates made fun of us or called us gay, was because they all knew why we did it. We were both talking to multiple girls at the same time, so if we went to homecoming with one of them, it would blow our cover with the others. We thought we were sly. But prom was different, so things started and things ended with other girls. I thought about her, and I knew I'd have to go all out to get her to come to prom with me.

After about six weeks of texting and hanging out, I took her to Spaghetti Works (her favorite restaurant), and asked her to prom in a cheese-typical way. She said yes! We were not dating but we were going to prom together. I was on my best behavior for the next month or so, and eventually convinced her to be my girlfriend. Ever since, I've been a "pretty good boy," and I'm proud to say I've never cheated since that revolving door time. That was six-plus years ago. The main reason for that was Superstar.

✶✶✶

I'm guessing you can relate to some of this, because we all have to go through these difficult growing up years. Hopefully, I can take what I've learned from this and use it to help kids who are faced with these same things. Peer pressure can be so strong, but we always have a choice. I guess I didn't really understand that then, but I want them to know that no matter what, we always have a choice.

Soon I went off to college and struggled with many other things. It was a new environment, 1,700 miles away from home. All of college was just a blur to me. I never thought it went by fast as they were the longest days of my life. Looking back, it's just one big blur. In college, I got serious about getting to the NFL. I trained all the time and graduated early so I could train for the draft. I didn't drink or smoke. I just wanted to win football games and Pac-12 titles.

My biggest faith test in college was when I tore my ACL in 2015. First game of the year, I had just been named a starter. I had a good first quarter in the game, and boom! A player chipped me from the side as I was planting, and I tore my knee. I'm not going to go into details about that experience, because it would take a very long time. Long story short, I was lost, on my own, living by myself, not part of the team. It was terrible, and the longest time in my life. I was depressed, but I remained faithful, and God was there with me the whole time. After overcoming that injury physically, and getting out of depression mentally, I found my favorite Bible verse:

> *Consider it pure joy, my brothers and sisters, whenever you face trials of many kinds, because you know that the testing of your faith produces endurance. Let endurance finish its work so that you may be mature and complete, not lacking anything.*
> *(James 1: 2-4)*

The great things about this verse are what I learned from a Pastor of mine. He taught me that the Hebrew translation for the word "testing" translates to a testing process the silversmith would use back in those days—the process of creating pure silver. For those of you who don't already know, the process starts by taking a bunch of silver and some metal pieces and throwing them into a cauldron. He would then heat the metal until it turns into a liquid. During this time, all the blemishes, plaque, and scum rise to the top layer of the liquid. The silversmith then wipes off the top layer with all of this scum. He cools down the metal, then heats it back up, and does the whole thing again. He does this over and over and over again. He scrapes the scum off, then looks at the liquid to see how much more he needs to do. Slowly, slowly, the metal becomes purer.

The silversmith knows he has 100% pure silver when he looks into the liquid and sees a direct reflection of himself, like he's looking into a mirror. In the same way, God keeps testing us. He throws all these crazy things into our lives, and heats it up. He wants to see if we keep our faith no matter what life kicks us with. Each time you have something unwanted in life, it's just a test of the faith. When you overcome the situation and stay faithful the entire time, God sees a reflection of Himself in you. We go through countless trials and tribulations through life with the goal that when it's time to meet our Maker, He can look down and see a direct reflection of Himself in you. That's what got me through that injury, and every struggle and trial since.

~4~

WHY I AM PASSIONATE ABOUT PAYING IT FORWARD

There aren't many better feelings in life than when someone does you a favor unexpectedly. Have you ever been in line at a drive-through and when you pull up to pay, the cashier informs you that the car in front of you paid for your items? I'm not a coffee drinker, but I've heard that many people have experienced this at a coffee store. The person in front of them pays for both of the drinks. It's such a warm feeling.

As much as I enjoy being on the receiving end of something like this, it's much greater to be the one who is giving. Paying it forward is one of the best ways to live life. We often forget how blessed we all are in life. No matter what your situation is, you can always pay it forward in some way. To explain why paying it forward is so important to me, I still look to my favorite Bible verse James 1: 2-4, mentioned above.

That verse was so powerful and life-changing for me, I have it tattooed on my left arm. Other than the fact that this helps me get through all the chaos in my life, it's also a great reminder that we should try to be God-like. Be a reflection of Christ. And how did Christ live? Just one reading of the New Testament, and Jesus paying it forward and serving others is engraved in your brain. What better way to serve the Lord than to serve others? That in itself gives enough motivation and passion to serve.

As if that wasn't enough, I also have a mother with a huge heart. She instilled in me how important it is to give back. She ran an at-home daycare for almost 20 years. She cared for each kid like they were my siblings. She also is constantly trying to help others. She's my mom-ager, as she calls it. Spoiled me my whole life. She's like this with everyone. Seeing her give her everything to these kids, family, and friends day in and out inspired me to serve now that I'm in my adulthood. Even with EVERYTHING I do now, she still calls and texts me, asking me to do more. She would give the shoes off her feet for someone in need.

It's easy to see the power and prestige the NFL brings. I still find myself caught up in being a fan, even though I'm a player. In no way am I famous, or a celebrity, but in Buffalo and in Omaha, I'd say people recognize my name. In Omaha, it's because of the success I had in high school, and because there are hardly any kids from Nebraska who get drafted to the NFL. In Buffalo, I gained some popularity because Pancho Billa drafted me, and because I was being compared to Kyle Williams, one of the greatest Bills in history. With or without that recognition, most people, and nearly every kid, think that if you're in the NFL, you're pretty cool. This makes it so easy to give back. I can go into the hospital and just walk door to door, pop in, talk about Bills football, and make someone's days.

Our platform gives us the perfect situation to give back. That's why I've visited Oishei Children's Hospital 30 plus times this last year. I even feel obligated to pay it forward. There have been hundreds of people who poured into me to get me where I am today. I can't write even half the names of the family, friends, teammates, and coaches who made me who I am today. You know who you are if you're reading this, and thank you! It's because of you guys that I want to serve others. You guys shaped me, pushed me, taught me, and molded me into the man I am today. I was given great people to be role models and help me, so I want to be a great role model now to others. You should want to be a great role model as well. You will never truly know how big of an impact you're having, but I promise, if you're paying it forward, it will be big enough.

Not all of these kids get the fortunate upbringing I had. We weren't wealthy or rich, probably lower middle class. My dad had bad luck with his job a few times. Company got bought out, or they were eliminating his position, things like that completely out of his control. Those made some times tougher than others, but they gave my sister and me anything we could've ever wanted. Took us to all sorts of sports, and we always had good equipment. It wasn't financial support that helped me, it was people genuinely caring for me and helping me get better. I want to be that supportive, reassuring voice to kids to help spark them to live the life they deserve! The world gets out of the way for people who know where they are going. I want to help them take the first step.

~5~

FAITH

My faith has been a rollercoaster. Perhaps yours has been, too. There have been many ups and downs, but I never truly lost faith. I was just less on fire for the Lord. There are consistencies with my faith. I never intentionally distance myself from the Lord, and I never stop praying. The distance happens when I prioritize other things first. It's so logical to spend more time thinking and working on a present issue than spending time working with Someone who is there for eternity.

For example, after my fourth season at Stanford, I decided I would declare for the NFL draft. Because I had a medical redshirt from my sophomore year, I technically had a fifth year of eligibility. After a record-setting year, and after much consulting and prayer, I decided to forego that season and enter the draft.

Immediately following the bowl game, I moved to San Diego—Carlsbad, to be exact. The NFL has a place there called Exos. This is where up to 50 of the best players in college go to train for the NFL combine. When I got my schedule, even I was shocked. I graduated early with two degrees, and still I was shocked at how many hours we trained.

Breakfast, lift, run drills, cardio, recovery. Lunch, short nap if you're lucky, position football drills, roll out, lift, run, dinner, study plays, take practice tests, call GF and Mom and Dad, sleep. Repeat six days a week. They were long, busy days, and when the break came, everyone just slept until about noon. Then we sat by the pool. During this time, faith was on the back burner. Again, I prayed every night, but I only read in my Bible or went to church about three times in six weeks.

Busy times are common in life. I'm sure buying or selling a house, a new job, a child, a new puppy—the list of stress-packed times in our lives can go on and on, but we always need to remain focused on what actually matters. This is one of my biggest struggles today. My logic is so flawed. I thought that because God's love endures forever, and because I have already been saved, there is a reserved place for me in heaven, so I can let earthly things be more important. It's not true. Even though Jesus' life was filled with stress, he often went away to be with God. I pray I can have the strength and patience to always put being God-like first in my life. I know it's hard, and I'll fail over and over again, but I must keep trying.

Another thing that I'm working on in my faith is keeping the Sabbath. Do you guys realize that almost all of us break one of the TEN COMMANDMENTS every week and not bat an eye? I never hear people talk about the Sabbath. For goodness sake, it's the third commandment! Out of all the sin in the world, God makes this the Third Commandment! He also teaches us that all sin is equal. What this really means is that all sins are offensive to God, because God demands perfection, and sin makes you imperfect. But still, you get the point. So I let the fact that Jesus' death and blood is enough to cover my sin, get the best of me.

I work every day. In my line of work, it's nearly impossible to take a fun 24 hours for Sabbath. I have not successfully done it yet. We play on Sundays, and our only true "off day" involves film, a lift, and recovery, if I want to be my best self on game day. In college, it was impossible because I genuinely had something mandatory every day of the week. And although Coach Shaw was a good guy, I don't think he would have let me out of classes and practice for my Sabbath day.

In high school, Sunday was my best bet, but with sports Friday and Saturday, Sunday was homework day and extra lift day. My whole adult life, I haven't kept the Sabbath, and worst of all, I never really try. I'd be interested in hearing some of your input on this. It's like a tornado in my head when I start thinking about it. When this happens to me, I think of another one of my favorite Bible verses:

> *I have fought the good fight, I finished the race,*
> *I have kept my faith.*
>
> *2 Timothy 4:7*

~6~

KIDS WITH SPECIAL NEEDS

Throughout my life there have been so many inspiring, caring, and incredible people I have met. It's been awesome getting to know the stories of these people. Out of all these heroes and mentors, the people who have impacted my life the most are the kids that I get to work with through my camps and activities in Harrison's Playmakers. From five years old, to 24 years old, these kids come in all shapes and sizes, with a plethora of different abilities! Each one of my kids teaches me more about life.

I have a strong memory of one of my sixth-grade lunches at Beadle Middle School. It was probably toward the middle of sixth grade after Christmas break when the class schedule had changed. This meant I had a different lunchtime with different people. That first day back after break, I strolled into the lunchroom to wait in line and order my lunch, which was normally a double or triple lunch.

When I got my food and turned to find a table to sit at, my group of friends were at a table that was completely full, so I looked around the lunchroom and saw a group of kids with special needs sitting together and eating with their teacher. I walked over and took a seat with them. I was very comfortable with these kids. My mom's at-home daycare when I was growing up had many different kids, with many different abilities. I had great relationships with friends who had Down syndrome, autism, and other intellectual disabilities. So sitting down that day at lunch, I was eager to meet new friends, and that's exactly what happened. I ended up sitting by Alex and Tyler who became good friends, too. After lunch we went into the gym for our 20-minute break and shot some hoops with the guys—

something they normally wouldn't have done if I didn't invite them. I thought nothing of this other than I was happy to make new friends. It was later that day when one of our teachers who works with the middle school's special needs students pulled me aside and let me know how much she appreciated my hanging out and playing with Alex and Tyler. It was my pleasure. I was happy to share laughs and be around so much positivity.

I made that lunch part of my routine clear into my middle school years. Some days I'd sit with my football teammates and hang with them, some days my wrestling teammates, and some days with Alex, Tyler, and their classmates. Tyler actually lived in my neighborhood. Over the summer, if he was ever outside when I was riding my bike, I'd stop and shoot hoops with him. By our eighth-grade bon voyage dance, Alex and Tyler were close with all of my friends, and we stole the show at the dance. I was proud to call them my friends.

When I was in high school, Unified sports wasn't quite a thing yet. It was just starting the year after I graduated. For those of you who don't know, Unified sports are inclusive sports that involve kids from Special Olympics playing alongside other kids without intellectual disabilities. It's an amazing initiative that Harrison's Playmakers follows, too. Now my high school has been recognized as a Unified banner school, meaning they are top in the state at inclusion. I was asked to come back to my school and give a speech during the banner presentation. I was extremely honored to do so. I look forward to more schools, and more states, getting involved in this.

In a way, Harrison's Playmakers is similar to Unified sports, and we are also similar to Special Olympics. We share many things with normal sports teams; however we are also different. The mission for Harrison's Playmakers is to promote social inclusion and the act of paying it forward with our Playmakers pups. Through mentorship, our year-round activities, inclusion, and my big football camp, we want to give these kids the opportunity to play sports and be on teams they may never have the option to do without us. Learning about celebrating others' success, failing and getting back up, courage, making new friends, joy, increased physical fitness, competition, and teamwork are just a small list of what we do.

We want all kids to practice, learn, and know that regardless of your different abilities, you can always find a way to help others. And that's what being a Harrison's Playmaker is all about.

My first Playmakers event was held in the Buffalo Bills indoor facility in May of 2019. With only three weeks of planning, we had over 125 people there for camp—about 60 kids with developmental differences, about 30 at-risk youth, and another 30 volunteers from the City of Good Neighbors (a Buffalo slogan).

I learned that what we are doing is very meaningful and impactful work. We're not just making a fun day for kids, we're changing lives. Our Omaha camp in 2019 was the gold standard for how our camps can and should run. 200 people got together for Harrison's Playmakers camp. It was miraculous.

Camp ran from 8:30 AM check-in until about 1:30 PM, but kids stayed around for pictures and autographs afterward. When we checked in our kids, they all received a tee shirt to wear for camp and breakfast. After everyone arrived, we had them run down a tunnel of all our volunteers, cheering and encouraging the kids, to get the juices flowing. I spoke to the kids, as did Greg, and then we did our Playmakers warm-up, which is really just a big dance to the electric slide. Next we split the kids up into smaller, more manageable, groups.

Kids in our camp range from a 13-year-old quarterback who may one day play in college, to kids who have never held a football before. We believe—no matter what your ability is—that you can participate in every station at your own capacity. For our kiddos who need a little more attention, we have one-on-one pairing with one of our volunteers. Aside from that, each station has a group leader running the show, and around four high school football players to help with anything else at that station. We had a total of 10 stations total: running back station, receiver station, quarterback station, tackling, agility drills, tug of war, water balloon toss, photo booth, field goal/kicking, relay races.

We spend about 10 minutes at a station, then we rotate. After three rotations (30 minutes), we all come together, take a break, water up, cool down, and do a group activity. These would include demonstrations from a Police Officer and his horse and dog, or Firefighters explaining all of their gear and letting kids climb into their firetrucks. The kids love this, and it gives them a break from the hot turf. It will take a good three hours to get through all of the stations and our group stuff. After that, it's time for lunch. Kids will normally sit with other kids in the group they have now become friends with and hang out while they eat. I love this part of making new friends. We bring everyone back down to the field for the last of our group activities. We do a big relay race, and a big group tug-of-war. Lastly, Greg and I will wrap up with some closing statements, and then give out a bunch of awards. On the way out from camp, kids will all get goodie bags as icing on the cake.

I'm looking forward to building on these camps with that as the baseline. We can always find ways to improve, and new obstacles will come up every year. We will work through all of them, please just pray for no rain! The camps are so big, it gives us the opportunity to meet new faces and show them how much fun we can have together. In those few hours at camp, I see more smiles than I do after a Bills home game win! Maybe that was a little exaggeration, but you get the point. Parents, volunteers, and, most importantly, the kids are so happy and full of joy. Being able to see that makes me want to keep going. Another favorite part of camp for me is when children surprise themselves by how much they can do. Last year, one of our pups who has Down syndrome told me she could never kick the ball over the field goal post. We worked with her, gave lots of help, and countless tries. After it was all said and done, she did it! Her clapping and jumping up and down not only made her mom cry, it brought a happy tear to my eyes as well.

Like I mentioned above, each camp gives us new faces. This is huge for us, because we don't just want to be a "one and done" camp every year. We want to see these kids over and over again throughout the year. Even with my busy schedule, I would like to at least meet up for similar events four to five times annually in each city. Unfortunately, I was injured and couldn't make it home as much as I would have normally, but we have done six or seven events in Buffalo in one year, so we know it's do-able. We believe it is crucial for these kids to get opportunities to make friends and be social outside of school. We provide another platform for this to happen organically. A fun one I do with the kids is to rent out Dave and Busters. The kids love it. Get them a card with unlimited swipes and some food and they didn't care who I was or what I wanted to talk to them about. They just wanted to go and play some games!

We've done a lot and can replicate this in Omaha and Sacramento as well. We brought a ton of our kids to one of my games, and got them on the field to meet some players. I would love to be able to pay for some of our Omaha and Sac kids to fly out and see me, too. We can also wait until we play closer to those cities (San Fran and Kansas City) and bus the kids and their families. The possibilities are endless.

What separates us from other camps is our big push to give back and pay it forward. Our volunteers are in this 100%, and we love them for it. But what does it look like for our kids to give back? So many times, people today see someone with special needs or different abilities and they assume that person isn't able to do much on their own, let alone do something for others. This isn't true. Everyone has their own abilities and can contribute positively to society. We try to find the best way for our kids to do that, and work from there. After talking to my kids at Dave and Busters, we decided we wanted to do a toy drive for kids who wouldn't be getting any Christmas presents this year. So I organized a toy drive for a local hospital that specializes in genetic disorders. These toys were for children who have to live at the hospital their entire life, and most don't have any family. Our Playmakers kids went out and bought toys from lists I received from the hospital. Then we all got together for dinner and wrapped hundreds of presents, made hand-written cards, and sang Christmas carols. We delivered the presents the next day.

That is what we are all about. We want to have our kids giving back in any way that they can. I constantly have kids telling me they held the door open for all their classmates, or they helped a woman carry groceries to her car. They are learning how important it is to give back, and how simple it can be. Some of the kids even get competitive with each other over it. "I'm holding the door open."—"No, I am."

It was heartwarming to me when some of our kids came to help me out after I was injured this season. One pup aided me in filling up my ice wraps and walking them over to me, as I was on crutches and couldn't walk. Another group got together, and with some help from parents, baked me some delicious food and desserts. And lastly, a few pups helped me write thank you cards to people who wrote me condolences on my injury. (They all have way better handwriting than mine.) This—after only working with them for a year. Imagine how on fire for servanthood they will be in another year or two! That's what being a Playmaker is about. Next I want to team up with Habitat for Humanity and have Harrison's Playmakers help paint a house, or clean up an entire park. Omaha, Buffalo, Sacramento, look out! We're coming, we're ready to help, and we mean business.

A byproduct of the work I do is that I am starting to receive national attention for my work with kids with developmental differences and special needs. Last season I was recognized twice by the NFL and NFLPA for my Playmakers event during that week. In the last month, I have been requested to speak to kids with special needs at six different events. Last week, I was in Rochester speaking at the 2020 Special Olympics Winter State Games to over 2,500 people and 1,000 athletes. Next week, I'm flying to another speaking engagement to speak to another 400 kids. I tell them all about Playmakers and challenge them to be Playmakers, too. Coaches, parents, and all the people involved love what we're doing.

I'm often asked, "Harrison, what is your biggest accomplishment?" That question always reminds me of a book I read titled "Gridiron Genius" by Michael Lombardi. It mentions a story about Branch Rickey, who played in the MLB, then became a sports executive for MLB. He helped create the minor leagues, helped initiate baseball helmets, is in the Baseball Hall of Fame, and is the person responsible for breaking the color barrier in baseball by signing Jackie Robinson. His book tells about a day when Branch Rickey, at the age of 74, was no longer the general manager of the Pittsburgh Pirates. A media member asked him the same question I'm often asked about his biggest accomplishment. His response was, "It hasn't happened yet." That's how I feel about Harrison's Playmakers. I'm so optimistic about where we are going.

One question I get asked often is, "How do you treat the kids?" They don't mean this disrespectfully, but not everyone is familiar with kids with different abilities. Kids with special needs are crazy talented. As I mentioned above, you can see how much they contribute to society. One thing I love about working with these kids is their ability to focus. I swear, it's like the words out of my mouth are the most important things ever, with the attention they give me. It makes coaching and teaching so much easier. I have learned that my kids do their best when I break things down into small steps that seem much more manageable than the larger task. My kids also amaze me with their memories. Unfortunately, I have been hit too many times in the head to remember all the great details, names, places, and conversations that some of my kids can. I'm often jealous about it, especially if they call me out on something!

So I treat Harrison's Playmakers like I treat all kids, regardless of their abilities. I worry kids will get distracted, so I keep things exciting and fun. I worry the camp might be too long, so I make breaks. I worry that a kid will get hurt, so we have a nurse's tent. I worry it will be too hot, so we have extra water breaks and spray misters. I worry a kid might be rude to another kid, so I make sure we have a good ratio of volunteers to participants. I worry kids will not like what we're doing, so I keep things flexible. It's no different than any other group of kids I work with. They are talented and gifted, so don't let a bad perception change the way you think.

Another thing I appreciate about my Playmakers is the amount of positivity we have at our events. Encouragement and joy pour out of them. In my experience, they are less judgmental, and love all types of people. And one last thing I enjoy is how they each have their own unique way of seeing the world. Have a deep conversation with them, and see the depth you can go with these kids. Some of the best conversations in my life are with my Playmakers pups.

~7~

COACHING

Greg talks a lot about being a coach. He has so much experience, I understand why. Greg wants me to help him put on coaching clinics and show coaches the right way to go about it. Coaching coaches is a very important task. A saying I love is, "Teachers teach until the time is up, coaches coach until the skill is learned."

I believe Greg and I have an uncommon way to address why kids quit playing football, and we also want to address the obstacles that arise when coaching kids of many different backgrounds.

Along my journey, many people have said I should go into coaching. It probably comes up because I love football so much. It consumes me constantly. Enough friends, players, and coaches have seen this in me and tell me I'll probably coach after it's all said and done. I don't agree or disagree. What I will say about it every time is, "Well, the world does need more good coaches."

I know from experience what good and bad coaching looks like. I know what it feels like to have a coach who doesn't believe in you, or a coach who doesn't push you enough. I've had coaches who didn't care about the person I was, just the player. I've also had coaches who have changed my world because of the positive influence they had on me, and I've had everything in between.

As I mentioned earlier, I had an unreal village that aided me in getting to the NFL. One important piece to most athletes' stories is a few great coaches. Not ALL great coaches, but I sure had a few. My story is different because the better coaches I had didn't push me. Most of the time they pulled me back or slowed me down.

My first sport was wrestling; my coach there was more like a babysitter. At three or four, it was hard for me to even sit still, let alone learn moves. But these coaches kept it fun and encouraged me. No matter how many times I failed, they taught me how important it is to get back up.

This was huge for me because I sucked my first few years. I lost almost every match. I was the youngest kid, but I was a big kid, so I had to wrestle kids way older than me who weighed the same as me. I remember weighing 64 pounds when I was five, and having to wrestle a 10-year-old because he was the closest in weight. Yes, I got beat badly, but I still had a smile on, because the coaches found ways to give me positive reinforcement.

Soccer and baseball are fun, but not for me. I was too physical for soccer, and too impatient for baseball. My parents didn't let me play football until sixth grade. It killed me not playing sooner, but it all worked out okay. My team was the KWAA Chiefs. The team had my best friends on it, so it was a blast, but we sucked. My first year in Peewee football, we went 0-9, I think. At this point, I was a really good wrestler, close to undefeated most years, so you'd assume I hated this season with all the losing. Turns out it was the most fun season of my life up to that point. I was madly in love with the game, and a big thanks was to the coach, Dickie Matthews.

He made sure football was fun, and he was almost more of a friend than a coach. I stayed with this losing team for three years. I could have switched to winning programs, but Dickie made it too much fun to leave. I'm competitive, and am the first person to say "focus up" if people are slacking off at practice. That wasn't us. We worked hard. We just had smaller, less athletic kids. We practiced just like the 9-0 team. That's why I loved it. We worked very hard, conditioned, we were punished for mistakes, were held accountable for our job, and it was fun! It's so sad to see kids retiring from sports at such young ages now. It seems impossible to do these things right anymore. Either coaches are tough on you and you win, but it's not fun—or it's fun, but you don't win. There's no reason sports have to be a catch 22.

This was never the case for me in high school. Football and wrestling were obviously my main sports. I did track and field in the Spring just to stay in shape and help the school. The Millard West wrestling program wasn't anything spectacular. We had one state champion in 16 years. My freshman year, we named a new head coach to the program, Coach Tinsley. Our football team, on the other hand, was known as a successful program. We won 10 games and made the playoffs every year. Coach Pete ran the program. He was known around Omaha. Most people I talked to were and are scared of that man. They have a right to be. He is vocal, strict, demanding, and can be rude or disrespectful. This is because he genuinely cares. He is so passionate about winning that if a player is distracting us from that or not helping us, he will let you know loud and in your face. I like that about him. He calls you out when he has to. For this reason, many people don't like him. I didn't like him for a year or two, but the more I saw him coach, and the more I saw him build lifelong relationships with former players, I knew all the madness was out of love, not hate.

Although I wasn't Pete's biggest fan for a couple of years, I didn't fear him like some others. I fear God, that's it. Well, maybe snakes, too, but who doesn't fear snakes. Anyway, I didn't like Pete early on because he didn't give me a chance to play on Varsity as a freshman. He had an old stubborn rule that he did not allow freshmen to play on Varsity. That ticked me off. Pete kept me humble. He didn't aid me in recruiting. He hated when my name was in the paper, and once he told me, "You must be smoking something if you think you're going to play in the PAC 12." So guess what I did next—got a full ride to play in the PAC 12.

I think there's a method to his madness. I look back and am so appreciative that he made me get everything on my own. If I wanted a school to look at me, I had to do it on my own merit. It made me work harder, and it made the scholarships oh so much sweeter knowing it wasn't because of a connection my coach had.

Pete is a family man and is loyal. My class gave everything we had for four years trying to win a state title. We fell short, and I think—besides myself—Pete hurt the most from that. He loved the class of 2014, because we gave him all we had. He didn't have to yell and scream as much as for teams in the past. We were lucky our team bonded so well. Whenever I'm home, I still look at the senior football team photo and remember the unforgettable times playing with those guys. They gave everything they had. When you give your all to a coach, you have demanded his respect. That's the relationship our class had with Pete. Win, loss, or draw, there will be memories for life because that loyalty created love. I love Pete, and I believe he'd say the same. At least, I hope so.

Pete kept me on a very short leash for three and a half years. He only let me off the leash after three years of proof. I molded into a "team first, we before me" type of leader. He handed the team to me during my final season, and we did the thing together. He let me call some of my own plays, and when the game was on the line, he would tell me, "Go do what you gotta do." He trusted me, and he listened to me. It was the best year of football in my life.

My wrestling coach was different. Scott Townsley's coaching style was similar but different. He was equally demanding and disciplined, but he was supportive. If a wrestler's record was 4-26, and that wrestler was going to wrestle a state championship undefeated wrestler, Townsley would sit after practice and watch his film of the drill moves that wrestler used, trying to prepare his kid to win. We all knew he wouldn't win, but Townsley gave the kid his everything, regardless. He believed in everyone.

Townsley took over the program, and as a first-year coach had a very upperclassmen-driven team. He would allow you to be as good as you wanted. If you wanted it to be hard, if you wanted to be great, he would do anything to make that happen. On the contrary, if you were only wrestling because your parents made you, or you just wanted a letter jacket, if you wanted it easy and didn't care about winning, he just let you do your thing. From my point of view, those kids were dead to him. They were wasting mat space and coaching time. I don't think he would word it that way. He's a lot more politically correct, but you get the idea. I respected this. This can't really work in a team sport, but in wrestling, you can be good with only a few studs carrying the team.

There are two huge things Townsley did that I really appreciated. That's the reason I would do anything for him to this day:

> *He took me to one of the biggest national tournaments of all time. After my second state title, we wanted to see how good I really was. He took me to Virginia Beach Nationals and coached me to win a 75-man bracket and become a national champion.*

> *He listened to me, and allowed me to prepare for college football.*

My senior year I was head and shoulders better than the next heavyweight wrestler. At that point in my career, when I already knew football was my love, Townsley would let me train for football in the weight room half the week, and wrestle the other half. This paid dividends when I ended up playing my true freshman year at Stanford. Townsley letting me do that helped a ton, and I respect him for it. Because of this, in my off-seasons, I go back to my high school wrestling team and train with them. I try to teach them my favorite moves. It's one of my favorite ways to train. I told the high school kids day one, "If any of you score a point on me when we wrestle live, I'll give you $1,000 cash." Just a little motivation for the guys. I'm thankful to Townsley for allowing me to help out.

One last coach I want to write about is my trainer, Matt Richardson. Matt doesn't work for a school or a fancy training facility. He's just a very knowledgeable man who cared. Matt's full-time job is a firefighter, and a father to six kids—two biological, two adopted, and two fostered. Aside from being an amazing father and husband, he pushed me more than I ever thought possible.

COACHING | 129

As you already know, I love going above and beyond what's asked when training. When it says five reps, I do six. That's the way I lifted and trained. At least it was until I met Matt. I can't remember exactly how we started, but I think he messaged me on Facebook about getting some free training sessions in. I was a curious kid at the time, and because I was starting to make a name for myself, lots of strength and conditioning coaches would ask me to train with them. I knew they only wanted to train me so if I made it big time, they could brag and say they got me there, but I didn't care. I'd take the guys up on their offers and workout with them a week or two to learn new lifts and strategies in training. It was a way to collect information, then just go do it on my own.

***

I was planning to do the same thing with Matt, but it didn't end up that way. Similar to most young high school boys, I didn't like to lift lower body or run anywhere close to lifting upper body. So of course my first workout with this random dude, Matt, was a lower body lift. We did a bunch of new stuff I'd never done before, but better than the new stuff was how hard he pushed me. Not into unsafe positions, or risk of injury, but to absolute fatigue. I don't know how he did it, but he almost broke me. You know how people say, a person worked them so hard, he almost killed them? It's similar, but he pushed me so hard, I almost killed myself. He wasn't making me do ridiculous reps and weight, he just made me dig deep and find more in the tank.

The funny story about this first workout is after it finished. We did some core, and talked about the next time we could meet up. I was trying to play it cool, but I was HURTING. I tried to have the fastest conversation ever. "Yup, it was a good one. Thanks so much. I'll text you to workout later this week. Bye."

I grabbed my stuff and gimped out the door. I got to my car, barely, threw up, and caught a double leg cramp. I'm talking quads, glutes, hammies, calves. All of it. I was scared to drive. I walked over to the side of the building and hid as Matt left. I called my parents and had them come pick me up. I rode with one as the other drove my car home. It was wild. After I do one of these workouts with a trainer, they normally post something online about how they just worked with Harrison Phillips, and they made me better—yada yada. They'd text and call, begging to train again soon. Matt didn't. Matter of fact, Matt didn't even text me until I reached out to him. No photos, no posts, just work.

After that, I knew this was my guy. We trained together three to four times a week for the next three years, including every time I came home from college. Matt was the most dedicated coach I had. He was the one who made me envision all of my dreams, then work to get there. Nutrition, recovery, training, performance, everything—he was my guy. I never had someone pour so much into me without expecting anything in return. Out of all the things he did for my development, he should have had his name in the paper and been on the news every time I was. He turned a boy into a man strictly by humbling me under the weights.

I would say Matt is not a hedgehog, which is a good thing for a coach. I will expand on this more in our coaching clinics, but I believe there are hedgehogs and foxes. Hedgehogs have a single power tool and can complete one job brilliantly. They look at problems, and try to fix them the only way they know how. Foxes, on the other hand, have a whole toolbox. They can do good in many areas, and look at problems through whatever lens can solve it best. Foxes do better overall. Matt took this approach to developing me not only physically, but mentally and socially as well. I will be forever grateful for his influence.

I could write hundreds of pages on different coaches I've had. I have been lucky enough to have had some pretty notable coaches. Shannon Turley is one of the most popular strength coaches in that space. He showed me mental strength, and the benefits it can have on your overall life. In the NFL, my rehab and sports performance team consists of experts—Will Greenberg (Strength and Conditioning/Nutrition), Joe Micca (Physical Therapy), Mackenzie Marques (Athletic Training), and Jo Clubb (Sports Science). Each one coaches me on different aspects to get me back to the best version of myself. Not to mention I've played for award-winning head coaches, David Shaw and Sean McDermott. Like I said, I could write a book about these coaches and their influence on me. However, instead of elaborating on each of their strengths and areas for growth, I can tell you there is no one right way to coach.

Every player, every team, every situation is vastly different from the others. There might not be the perfect coach, but there are coaches who do things in ways that can harm, deter, and worsen a player, team, or situation. Through the coaching clinics Greg wants to run, I believe that we can give coaches tools and new ways of thinking that won't just make you better coaches, it will make youth sports ramp back up again. Last week, Ralph Wilson, the foundation director, told me that 65% of kids drop out of sports as young as age 12, and they don't return to sports. That's just in this area of western New York! That hurt my heart. We need to combat that problem and do it through proper coaching. Remember, if everyone is thinking alike, no one is thinking at all. Greg has a million ideas on how that can work, and I'll be there to shine my light on the matter, too.

CONCLUSION

These pages can't paint the perfect picture I was trying to show. I hope it gives you a little insight into a few things in my life—my background, my relationship with Roz, my faith, my shortcomings, my desire to work with my foundation, and the importance of coaching moving forward in youth sports. I want you to see that:

I have a relationship with Jesus Christ and try to honor Him. I have failed miserably and will continue to fall short, but my God knows my heart, and I'm working to be that reflection He wants to see.

The kids with developmental differences and special needs that I work with are the most amazing people I have ever spent time with. Harrison's Playmakers make me a better person, and inspire me every day. No one can put limits or ceilings on these kids. I have seen with my own eyes the good they do, and how much they care about giving back and paying it forward.

If you want to get involved in Harrison's Playmakers, just reach out. I read all the messages on social media you send. I check my e-mails and talk with my Playmakers team daily. I would love for you guys to get on board and learn more about the places God is working with us, and the places He's taking us. The future looks bright. If any of you are still reading, I applaud you!

Remember, even on your worst days, the good outweighs the bad. God Bless!

~ ~ ~ ~ ~ ~ ~

Harrison Phillips can be reached through these links:
Twitter: @horribleharry99
IG: Harrisonphillips99
Facebook: Harrison Phillips

PART THREE

RESOURCES

INVITE COACH ROZ TO SPEAK TO YOUR GROUP!

COACHING

Coach Roz and Harrison hold one-day coaching clinics around the country. Coach specializes in:
- Coaching for Character
- Building a youth program for tomorrow
- Reshaping your coaching model
- Transformational and relational coaching

FAITH BASED

Roz speaks in churches across the country on the following subjects:
- Faith outside the walls
- Your sports team IS your congregation
- Finishing your life well
- Transformation

CORPORATE

Coach is sought to speak at corporate functions in a fun, yet direct format, including:
- Changing the Culture
- Think "Team"
- Define a higher goal
- Creating Leaders
- Custom-Designed Presentations

Roz is humorous, yet direct, and to the point. He can reach the heart of the matter quickly. He encourages peer-to-peer mentoring, and believes your responsibility to yourself and your team is a high priority. He can speak to any group, whether it be CEOs, Pastors, or anyone else. His unique manner inspires his listeners to reach for new heights.

When you invite Coach Roz to speak to your group, he becomes part of your team, and you of his. To bring Coach Roz to your group, or your area, he can be reached through any of the links below:

Coach Roz Roeszler ~ 916-220-1284
E-mail: coachroz@theplaymakers.org
Website: www.theplaymakers.org
Blog: www.theplaymakers.wordpress.com
Twitter: Playmakers_org
IG: theplaymakersorg
Facebook: The Playmakers

COACHING FOR CHARACTER CLINICS

Our coaching clinics are designed for the coaches and volunteers who have the courage to look at their task in new and creative ways. Some of the topics we may be exploring together:

- The relationships that we've had with our Dads
- How sports has shaped our adult coaching
- Relational coaching
- Reshaping your coaching model
- Playmakers' core values

We invite you to become part of the Playmakers coaching model. This could include:

- Becoming eligible to receive a Playmakers coaching stipend
- Coaching at Playmakers camps around the country
- Your personal mission statement
- Organizational mission statement
- Forming a Playmakers location

Here is a clinic that could change your life, as well as the life of a child. Location is not a problem, as we hold our clinics all over the country.

Playmakers also serves as a Coach's Certification Center, providing the hours needed for Youth Coaching Certification.

If you would like to learn more about this unique way of coaching, or if you would like to bring a Coaching Clinic to your area, contact Coach Roz.

Coach Roz Roeszler ~ 916-220-1284
E-mail: coachroz@theplaymakers.org
Website: www.theplaymakers.org
Blog: www.theplaymakers.wordpress.com
Twitter: Playmakers_org
IG: theplaymakersorg
Facebook: The Playmakers

FREE SUMMER FOOTBALL CAMPS

I am a football coach in my core and have attended as many football camps as most of my coaching partners. I believe that I understand the "value" of most camps. Here is how our camps are unique:

1. They are designed for kids who may NEVER play football competitively.
2. Playmakers camps are FREE to everyone.
3. This opens you and your coaches to the bigger picture of kids with special challenges.
4. Your players will work together "helping others." This is team building at its best.
5. Your community will embrace your program when they see your program includes serving others.
6. Your staff will learn concepts that you may not be familiar with, such as:
   a. 1 hour and 15 minute practices
   b. Character built into your practice week
   c. Conditioning and tackling done the right way
   d. Preparing parents for your program
   e. The power of peer-to-peer mentoring

If you'd like to have a Playmakers camp in your area, we need a "core" person to help us get the ball rolling. What would that involve? Organizing pre-camp activities, and connecting Coach Roz with leaders in your community. Having a "point" person is key to our being able to come to a new area.

Volunteers are a necessary component at our camps. We need people to help with registration and check-in. We need people to set up the field, and man the water station. We always need a First Aid person and a trainer. We need a liaison who can link our efforts with the local law enforcement and the Fire Department. Many times people will donate food and other supplies, and make donations to help with the ongoing cost of these camps.

Together, we are making a difference. The world of tomorrow is in our children's hands. What better way to assure them a promising future than to offer them a program that offers hope and promise!

If you would like to bring a Playmakers Summer Football Camp to your area, contact Coach Roz. He would welcome your call.

Coach Roz Roeszler ~ 916-220-1284
E-mail: coachroz@theplaymakers.org
Website: www.theplaymakers.org
Blog: www.theplaymakers.wordpress.com
Twitter: Playmakers_org
IG: theplaymakersorg
Facebook: The Playmakers

PARTNERING WITH PLAYMAKERS

Playmakers is on a radical mission to use sports to transform youth today. We need partners who are committed to sacrificing their time and talents to invest in our kids. We need passionate people who are crazy about kids, team, and character. We are "old school" in that we believe we need to bring kids back to the basics of "it's not all about you." This is a mission worth the ride, and it is fun along the way. We need:

- Funding (Our dollars are stretched well, with no waste)
- Volunteers:
  - Admin
  - Grant writing
  - Social Media
  - Board members (regionally)
  - Mentors
  - Corporate partners
  - Event Planners
  - Project managers
  - Coaches

When you engage with Playmakers, you will see a model that can be duplicated across the country, and you could be part of that team.

The Playmakers program began in the Sacramento area. From there it spread throughout California, and is now reaching not only a national but also an international audience. There are many ways to be part of this rapidly growing program.

If you would like to volunteer in some capacity, or contribute whatever special talent you have in your own unique way, please know we would welcome it. Just let us know what you have in mind, and we'll find a way to plug you in.

The Playmakers philosophy can be applied in a variety of settings, including music and the arts. If that is your forte, let us know. We would be happy to help you get the Playmakers program up and running.

Playmakers is made up of many hands, many hearts, and many willing feet. We invite you to be among us.

Coach Roz Roeszler ~ 916-220-1284
E-mail: coachroz@theplaymakers.org
Website: www.theplaymakers.org
Blog: www.theplaymakers.wordpress.com
Twitter: Playmakers_org
IG: theplaymakersorg
Facebook: The Playmakers

Harrison Phillips can be reached through these platforms:
Twitter: @horribleharry99
IG: Harrisonphillips99
Facebook: Harrison Phillips

ABOUT PLAYMAKERS BOOKS

Greg "Coach Roz" Roeszler has dedicated his life to helping underprivileged, at-risk children, wherever they are. These books were born out of that passion. Written with wisdom, humor, and deep compassion, each book is certain to touch the heart of its readers. The concepts contained within these books apply to every aspect of life, not just the game of football. The books not only speak directly to their targeted audience, they offer deep insight to a general audience as well.

Many of the children Roz works with come from extremely difficult circumstances. Some are homeless, or parent-less, or father-less. Their story needs to be told, and solutions must be provided. Roz believes that at least some of the answers can be found within the kids themselves. Through the game of football, Roz teaches the kids to be accountable to each other, and to care about each other by being part of the football family. Slowly the kids have learned what it means to be a responsible citizen of their community, to help and serve others, and to reach beyond themselves simply because it was the right thing to do.

After seeing the difference this approach made with his own students, Coach Roz began working with coaches all over the State of California, teaching them how to coach character while coaching football. As his clinics increased in number, so did the need for a Coaching for Character Manual. In his own unique way, Coach Roz shows his readers how to focus on the deeper values that lie hidden within the game. It is Roz's premise that when taught correctly, the game of football can be a blueprint for life. *Coaching for a Bigger Win: A Playbook for Coaches*, contains that blueprint, at least in part.

Coach Roz works closely with the Mothers of his students, many of whom are single parents in need of guidance and encouragement. Roz makes a point of forming a team with these Moms not only to help them, but ultimately to help their child as well. Over time, Roz developed a repertoire of sayings that he used with his Moms. It was a natural extension for him to collect those sayings and put them in a book so they could be used as a reference. Thus, *Raising Your Student Athlete, A Playbook for Moms* was born.

Beyond Coaching goes deeper into what it means to be a relational coach, and how that affects all aspects of your life as a coach, husband, father, and mentor. Written out of the abundance of their hearts, this book comes from two men who have been able to connect with a larger vision for their lives. It is their hope, and their prayer, that this book will inspire you to join the Playmakers network of coaches and volunteers who use the great game of football to touch the lives of many deserving kids and families.

ORDER MORE BOOKS

Coaching Character and Leadership: A Playbook for Parents
Coaching for a Bigger Win: A Playbook for Coaches

Price: $12.95 x _____ (number of copies) $ _____

Case of 24: $300 x _____ (number of cases) $ _____

Sales Tax (7% when shipped to Nebraska addresses only) $ _____

Shipping & Handling: $5 per book, $25 per case   Total $ _____

Beyond Coaching: Building Character and Leadership

Price: $19.95 x _____ (number of copies) $ _____

Case of 12 : $200 x _____ (number of cases) $ _____

Sales Tax (7% when shipped to Nebraska addresses only) $ _____

Shipping & Handling: $5 per book, $25 per case   Total $ _____

Customer Name: _____

SHIP TO Address: _____

City: _____ State: _____ Zip: _____

Telephone: (____) _____

Email: _____

Payment Method:

☐ Visa   ☐ Master Card   ☐ American Express   ☐ Discover

Name on Card: _____

BILL TO Address (if different from above): _____

City: _____ State: _____ Zip: _____

Card Number: _____ CVV: _____

Total Amount to be Charged: _____

Signature: _____ Exp. Date: _____

Mail This Form To:
Playmakers Press
c/o CMI Fulfillment
4822 South 133rd Street, Omaha, NE 68137
E-mail: playmakers@conciergemarketing.com
Or order online at: *www.ThePlaymakers.org*

ACKNOWLEDGMENTS

Linda Freeman Roeszler

In our first two books, I had the opportunity to thank many people. They included coaches, pastors, family, and my heroes. There are many to thank with this book as well, but this time I particularly want to acknowledge one person—my best friend and wife of 26 years—Linda Louise.

Lou, you are first a beautiful woman of God. You have given me the freedom to pursue this dream of Playmakers. You have prepared countless beds for kids on our couch. You have fed, mothered, and prayed for so many kids. You have given up so many summer vacations, and sat in almost empty bleachers cheering for kids who do not get cheered for. You do so much for so many who will never know where it came from. You just amaze me. Without you, I am lost, but you keep us moving forward. Thank you for being Mrs. Coach Roz, my wife and family ambassador. Thank you for encouraging me when I get scared and am in over my head. You are the family Playmaker. Now let's see what's in store for us in the next 30 years. That will get us to 90, and we can see what happens from there. I love you, Lou.

…Roz

Harrison Phillips and Greg "Coach Roz" Roeszler

ABOUT THE AUTHORS

Greg Roeszler's passion for lost and forgotten kids caused him to leave a successful career in the business sector so he could devote his life to working with at-risk kids. As Greg puts it, "I am a football coach, a husband, and a dad struggling to be the man I have been called to be." Out of that calling, Playmakers Mentoring Foundation was born. Supported early on by a network of coaches and friends who shared his vision, Playmakers currently reaches throughout the State of California, and has chapters in Buffalo, New York, and Omaha, Nebraska.

Greg, his wife, Linda, and their two daughters live in Sacramento, California. For more information about Playmakers, please go to www.theplaymakers.org.

~ ~ ~ ~ ~ ~ ~

Harrison Phillips was drafted as a Defensive Tackle for the Buffalo Bills after having graduated from Stanford University in 3-½ years with two degrees. His outstanding achievements and awards, both academically and athletically, have certainly set him apart from most people, but his great heart for the lost and forgotten is what makes him unique. Harrison works tirelessly with numerous charitable organizations, but his great love is visiting the children's hospitals in whatever city he happens to be in. Harrison is on the Playmakers Board of Directors and works closely with Coach Roz in developing the Playmakers outreach. We are grateful to have him on the Playmakers team. Harrison is from Omaha, Nebraska.

Donna Miesbach with her great-grandson, Eli.

Donna Miesbach's inspirational poems and articles have spanned the globe for the past 35 years through such venues as *Unity Magazine, Daily Word, Contemplative Journal,* and *Christian Living in the Mature Years.* She is the author of the award-winning book, *From Grief to Joy: A Journey Back to Life & Living.* She is also the retired assistant to Coach Greg Roeszler, Founder & Executive Director of Playmakers Mentoring Foundation. Donna co-authors all of Playmakers' Books.

In addition to her writing, Mrs. Miesbach was certified as a meditation and yoga instructor through the Chopra Center for Well Being in California. She lives and works in Omaha, NE, where she enjoys her children, grandchildren, and many great-grandchildren.